ERRORS OF OBSERVATION
AND THEIR TREATMENT

ERRORS OF OBSERVATION AND THEIR TREATMENT

by

J. TOPPING, Ph.D., F.Inst.P.

Formerly Vice-Chancellor, Brunel University

FOURTH EDITION

LONDON   NEW YORK

CHAPMAN AND HALL

First published 1955
Second edition 1957
Third edition 1962
Fourth edition 1972 *by*
Chapman and Hall Ltd
11 New Fetter Lane, London EC4P 4EE
Published in the USA by
Chapman and Hall
733 Third Avenue, New York NY 10017
Reprinted twice
Reprinted 1979, 1984

© 1972 *J. Topping*

Printed in Great Britain by
J. W. Arrowsmith Ltd., Bristol

ISBN 0 412 21040 1

PREFACE

This little book is written in the first place for students in technical colleges taking the National Certificate Courses in Applied Physics; it is hoped it will appeal also to students of physics, and perhaps chemistry, in the sixth forms of grammar schools and in the universities. For wherever experimental work in physics, or in science generally, is undertaken the degree of accuracy of the measurements, and of the results of the experiments, must be of the first importance. Every teacher of experimental physics knows how "results" given to three or four decimal places are often in error in the first place; students suffer from "delusions of accuracy." At a higher level too, more experienced workers sometimes claim a degree of accuracy which cannot be justified. Perhaps a consideration of the topics discussed in this monograph will stimulate in students an attitude to experimental results at once more modest and more profound.

The mathematical treatment throughout has been kept as simple as possible. It has seemed advisable, however, to explain the statistical concepts at the basis of the main considerations, and it is hoped that Chapter 2 contains as elementary an account of the leading statistical ideas involved as is possible in such small compass. It is a necessary link between the simple introduction to the nature and estimation of errors given in Chapter 1, and the theory of errors discussed in Chapter 3. Proofs have usually been omitted but references to other works are given in the text. There is also a list of books for further reading.

I am much indebted to other writers, which will be obvious, and to many groups of students particularly those at The Polytechnic, Regent Street, London, who bore patiently with my attempts to get them to write every experimental result as $x \pm y$. I am also much indebted to friends and old students who have helped me with the provision of suitable data, and I am specially grateful to Mr. Norman Clarke, F.Inst.P., Deputy Secretary of The Institute of Physics, who has kindly read the manuscript and made many helpful suggestions.

The author of a book of this kind must always hope that not too many errors, accidental or personal, remain.

Acton   J. TOPPING
    July, 1955.

PREFACE TO THIRD EDITION

Opportunity has been taken to make one or two corrections and a few slight additions.

I am grateful to all those who have written and made suggestions. It is pleasing that the book has found acceptance in universities and other institutions, both in this country and overseas.

J. TOPPING

Brunel College of Technology,
   London, W.3.
      October, 1961.

PREFACE TO FOURTH EDITION

With the adoption by Britain of the system of S.I. units appropriate changes have been made throughout the book.

Some other small revisions have also been made.

October, 1971.   J. TOPPING

CONTENTS

CHAPTER 1

ERRORS OF OBSERVATION

"And so we see that the poetry fades out of the problem, and by the time the serious application of exact science begins we are left with only pointer readings."

EDDINGTON

1. Accidental and systematic errors

Although physics is an exact science, the pointer readings of the physicist's instruments do not give the exact values of the quantities measured. All measurements in physics and in science generally are inaccurate in some degree, so that what is sometimes called the "accurate" value or the "actual" value of a physical quantity, such as a length, a time interval or a temperature, cannot be found. However, it seems reasonable to assume that the "accurate" value exists, and we shall be concerned to estimate limits between which this value lies. The closer these limits the more accurate the measurement. In short, as the "accurate" value is denied us, we shall endeavour to show how the "most accurate" value indicated by a set of measurements can be found, and how its accuracy can be estimated.

Of course the aim of every experimentalist is not necessarily to make the error in his measurements as small as possible; a cruder result may serve his purposes well enough, but he must be assured that the errors in his measurements are so small as not to affect the conclusions he infers from his results.

The difference between the observed value of any physical quantity and the "accurate" value is called the **error of observation.** Such errors follow no simple law and in general arise from many causes. Even a single observer using the same piece of apparatus several times to measure a certain quantity will not always record exactly the same value. This may result from some lack of precision or uniformity of the instrument or instruments used, or from the variability of the observer, or from some small changes in other physical factors which control the measurement. Errors of observation are usually grouped as **accidental** and **systematic.** although it is sometimes difficult to distinguish between them and many errors are a combination of the two types.

Accidental errors are usually due to the observer and are often revealed by repeated observations; they are disordered in their incidence and variable in magnitude, positive and negative values occurring in repeated measurements in no ascertainable sequence. On the other hand, systematic errors may arise from the observer or the instrument; they are usually the more troublesome, for repeated observations do not necessarily reveal them and even when their existence or nature has been established they are sometimes difficult to eliminate or determine; they may be constant or may vary in some regular way. For instance, if a dial gauge is used in which the pivot is not exactly centred, readings which are accurately observed will be subject to a periodic systematic error. Again, measurements of the rise of a liquid in a tube using a scale fixed to the tube will be consistently too high if the tube is not accurately vertical; in this case the systematic errors are positive and proportional to the height of liquid. Further, measuring devices may be faulty in various ways; even the best possible instruments are limited in precision and it is important that the observer should appreciate their imperfections.

Errors peculiar to a particular observer are often termed **personal** errors; we sometimes speak of the "personal equation." Errors of this kind are well authenticated in astronomical work. Bessel, for instance, examined the estimates of time passages in astronomical observations and found that systematic differences existed amongst the leading astronomers of his time. That similar differences exist amongst students and observers today will be familiar to teachers and scientific workers alike.

More fundamentally there is the "error" introduced by the very process of observation itself which influences in some measure the phenomenon observed. In atomic physics this is specially important and is enshrined in the uncertainty principle due to Heisenberg, but in macroscopic phenomena with which we shall be mainly concerned it can be neglected. Further, there are many phenomena in physics, often included under the general term "noise," where fluctuations arise due to atomic or sub-atomic particles which set a natural limit to the accuracy of measurements. These fluctuations are, however, usually very much smaller than the errors which arise from other causes. For instance, molecular bombardments of the suspension of a suitably sensitive galvanometer produce irregular deflexions which can be recorded. An example of such deflexions obtained using a torsion balance is shown in Fig. 1.

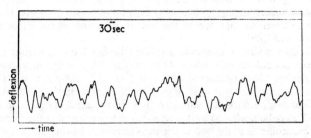

Fig. 1.   Record of the deflexions of a supersensitive torsion balance showing irregular fluctuations in time due to the Brownian motion of the instrument.   (From an investigation by E. Kappler.)

2. Errors and fractional errors

If a quantity x_0 units is measured and recorded as x units we shall call $x - x_0$ the **error** in x_0, and denote it usually by e. It might be positive or negative but we shall assume throughout that its numerical value is small compared with that of x_0; this is usually written $|e| \ll |x_0|$.

We can write

$$x = x_0 + e$$
$$= x_0(1 + f)$$

where $f = e/x_0$ and is known as the **fractional error** in x_0. Also $100e/x_0$ is called the **percentage error** in x_0. Of course e/x_0 can be written as e/x approximately when $|e| \ll |x_0|$, that is, when $|f| \ll 1$.

We note that
$$\frac{x}{x_0} = 1 + f$$

and
$$\frac{x_0}{x} = \frac{1}{1 + f} \simeq 1 - f \quad \text{if} \quad |f| \ll 1$$

Also,
$$\frac{e}{x_0} = \frac{e}{x} \cdot \frac{x}{x_0} = \frac{e}{x}(1 + f) \simeq \frac{e}{x}$$

11

3. Estimate of error

If only a single measurement is made any estimate of the error may be widely wrong. There may be a large personal or accidental error, as well as that due to the lack of precision of the particular instrument used.

To take a simple example, a student timing the oscillations of a simple pendulum may count 49 swings as 50, and the stop-watch he uses may be accurate to perhaps $0·1$ second. Also his "reaction time," in using the stop-watch, may be different from that of another student, but perhaps in a timing such as this the effect of the "reaction time" may be neglected as it is reasonable to assume it is the same at the beginning as at the end of the time interval. In this case, assuming he counts the swings correctly the error in the measurement is dictated by the accuracy of the stop-watch. The fractional error in the timing may be reduced by increasing the number of swings timed but this tends to increase the error in counting the number of swings, unless some counting device is used. The following times were obtained by ten different students using the same pendulum and the same watch: $37·2$, $37·0$, $36·9$, $36·7$, $36·8$, $36·2$, $35·4$, $37·2$, $36·7$, $36·8$ seconds for 20 swings and $73·8$, $74·3$, $74·0$, $74·2$, $74·4$, $74·0$, $74·1$, $73·6$, $74·7$ seconds for 40 swings.

To obviate or reveal accidental errors, repeated measurements of the same quantity are made by the same observer, whenever possible. (If the phenomenon is unique the measurements cannot be repeated; for example, we cannot repeat the measurements of an eclipse. Of course in a fundamental sense all measurements are unique; they all refer to a particular instant.) A set of repeated measurements might be $10·1$, $10·0$, $10·0$, $10·2$, $12·3$, $10·1$, $10·1$, $10·0$, $10·1$, $10·2$. It seems quite possible that some mistake was made in recording $12·3$ and it is reasonable to reject it on these grounds. (Results should however not be rejected indiscriminately or without due thought. Abnormal or unusual results, followed up rather than discarded, have in the hands of a great scientist often led to important discoveries.) The above measurements indicate that the measured quantity lies between $10·0$ and $10·2$, and as the arithmetic mean of the nine measurements is $10 + (1/9)(0·8) \simeq 10·1$, we can say that the measured quantity is $10·1 \pm 0·1$ to indicate the scatter of the measurements about the mean. In fact, in stating that the value of the measured quantity is $10·1$ the numerical error is likely

12

to be less than $0 \cdot 1$, and indeed it is possible on certain reasonable assumptions to calculate the probability that the error is not greater than some assigned magnitude. We shall discuss this more fully later.

We note here that if a quantity x_0 units is measured n times and recorded as $x_1, x_2, - - - x_n$ units, we can write $x_r = x_0 + e_r$ where e_r is the **error** in the measurement x_r. The arithmetic mean $\bar{x}$ of the n measurements is

$$\bar{x} = \frac{x_1 + x_2 + \cdots + x_n}{n} = x_0 + \frac{e_1 + e_2 + \cdots + e_n}{n}$$

and as some of the errors $e_1, e_2, - - - e_n$ may be positive and some negative the value of $(e_1 + e_2 + \cdots + e_n)/n$ may be very small. In any case it must be smaller numerically than the greatest value of the separate errors.

Thus if e is the largest numerical error in any of the measurements we have

$$\left| \frac{e_1 + e_2 + \cdots + e_n}{n} \right| \leqslant e$$

and consequently $|\bar{x} - x_0| \leqslant e$.

Hence in general $\bar{x}$ will be near to x_0 and may be taken as the "best" value of the measured quantity which the measurements provide. In general the larger the value of n the nearer $\bar{x}$ approaches x_0.

It will be noticed that it is not possible to find $e_1, e_2, - - - e_n$ or e since x_0 is not known. It is usual therefore to examine the **scatter** or **dispersion** of the measurements not about x_0 but about $\bar{x}$. We shall discuss this more fully later, but if we write $x_r = \bar{x} + d_r$, then d_r denotes the deviation of x_r from $\bar{x}$: it is sometimes called the **residual** of x_r.

We have $\qquad x_r = x_0 + e_r = \bar{x} + d_r$

so that $\qquad e_r - d_r = \bar{x} - x_0$

and $\qquad e_1 + e_2 + \cdots + e_n = n(\bar{x} - x_0)$

whereas $\qquad d_1 + d_2 + \cdots + d_n = 0$.

We note then that by repeated measurements of the same quantity accidental errors of the observer may be corrected in some degree, but systematic errors peculiar to him *cannot* thus be obviated nor can any lack of accuracy in the instrument itself. To take an

13

obvious example, with a scale wrongly marked as 9 instead of 10 an observer might record measurements of $9 \cdot 0$, $9 \cdot 1$, $9 \cdot 0$, - - - instead of $10 \cdot 0$, $10 \cdot 1$, $10 \cdot 0$, - - - and the arithmetic mean of the former readings, however many there be, will have a "systematic" error of $1 \cdot 0$. This example is not so absurd as at first sight it may seem, for every instrument records m instead of M where $M - m$ or $(M - m)/M$ is a measure of the accuracy of the instrument. It is important that the observer should know what degree of accuracy he can achieve with the instrument he is using. Indeed this information helps him to decide whether the instrument is the right one to use, whether it is appropriate to the particular end he has in view.

How accurately can a length of about 50 cm be measured using a metre rule? Is this sufficiently accurate for the purpose? If not, should a cathetometer be used? These are the sort of questions which any scientist must ask and answer. The answers to these questions dictate the experimental apparatus he uses. It is of little avail measuring one quantity with an accuracy of 1 in 1000, say, if another quantity which affects the result equally can only be measured with an accuracy of 1 in 100.

Here the distinction that is drawn between the terms *accuracy* and *precision* might be noted.* *Accuracy* refers to the closeness of the measurements to the "actual" value or the "real" value of the physical quantity, whereas the term *precision* is used to indicate the closeness with which the measurements agree *with one another* quite independently of any systematic error involved. Using the notation introduced earlier in this section we say that a set of measurements x_1, x_2 - - -, x_n are of high precision if the residuals d_r are small whatever the value of $\bar{x} - x_0$, whereas the accuracy of the measurements is high if the errors e_r are small in which case $\bar{x} - x_0$ is small too. Accuracy therefore includes precision but the converse is not necessarily true. Sometimes more is known of the precision of an instrument than of its accuracy.

It will be clear that the assessment of the possible error in any measured quantity is of fundamental importance in science. It involves estimating (*a*) the accidental error, (*b*) the systematic or personal error of the observer, and (*c*) the systematic error of the

* I am grateful to Dr. H. S. Peiser who kindly brought to my notice Dr. Churchill Eisenhart's article in *Photogrammetric Engineering*, Vol. XVIII, No. 3, June 1952.

instrument. Of these the accidental error is usually assessed by applying certain statistical concepts and techniques as we shall explain in Chapter 2. The other two errors, (b) and (c), are sometimes merely neglected or are assumed to be smaller than (a) which is not always true. Indeed systematic errors are often the most serious source of inaccuracy in experimental or observational work and scientists have to devote much time and care to their elimination and estimation. Various devices are used depending upon the nature of the measurements and of the apparatus used. There is no common or infallible rule. Certain systematic errors may be eliminated by making the measurements in special ways or in particular combinations; others may be estimated by comparing the measurements with those obtained when a quite different method or different instrument is employed. On the other hand the personal error of an observer is usually treated as constant and is determined by direct comparison with an automatic recording device or with the results of other observers. Once determined it is used to correct all the readings made by the observer. Various other corrections may be applied to the readings to take account of estimated systematic errors. In all cases the aim is so to correct the readings as to ensure that all the errors remaining are accidental. Sometimes the experiments are so designed and the measurements so randomized that any remaining systematic errors acquire the nature of accidental errors. This device is used particularly in many biological experiments.

Of course, even when all this has been done systematic errors sometimes remain. Birge has pointed out, for instance, that "atomic weight determinations prior to 1920 were afflicted with unknown and unsuspected systematic errors that averaged fully ten times the assumed experimental errors." Also, the history of the measurement of fundamental physical constants such as the velocity of light, the electronic charge and Planck's constant records how various systematic errors have been revealed and corrected. For example, in 1929 the accepted value of the electronic charge was $4 \cdot 7700 \times 10^{-10}$ e.s.u.; later it was revised to $4 \cdot 8025 \times 10^{-10}$ e.s.u., the difference between these two values being much greater than the accepted accidental error of the earlier value.

Students are recommended to read some of the accounts, particularly the original papers, of experimental work of high accuracy. If one instructive example may be selected, E. C. Bullard[1] has discussed some gravity measurements made in East Africa. After examining very carefully both the accidental and systematic errors involved he concludes that the measurements form a consistent set with a probable error of about $0.000\ 01\ \text{ms}^{-2}$. However, he cautiously adds: "While it is believed that the discussion of the errors includes all those large enough to be of any practical importance it must be remembered that many apparently irreproachable gravity measurements have in the past been found to be subject to unexpected and unexplained errors, and until the source of these discrepancies has been found it would be unwise to be dogmatic about the errors in the present work."

4. Estimate of the error in compound quantities

Once the error in a measured quantity has been estimated it is a fairly simple matter to calculate the value of the consequential error in some other quantity on which it depends.

If y is some function of a measured quantity x, the error in y due to some error in x can be found by using some simple mathematical techniques which we shall now explain.

5. Error in a product

If a quantity Q is expressed as the product of ab, where a and b are measured quantities having fractional errors f_1 and f_2 respectively, we can write

$$Q = ab$$
$$= a_0(1 + f_1) \times b_0(1 + f_2)$$
$$\simeq a_0 b_0(1 + f_1 + f_2)$$

so that the fractional error in Q is $f_1 + f_2$ approximately, that is, the sum of the fractional errors in the two quantities of which Q is the product.

EXAMPLE

If the measured lengths of the sides of a rectangle have errors of 3% and 4%, the error in the calculated value of the area is 7% approximately, if the errors in the sides have the same sign, or 1% if they have opposite signs.

16

The above result can easily be extended. First we note that by putting $a = b$ it follows that the fractional error in a^2 is twice the fractional error in a. Alternatively, the fractional error in a is one-half the fractional error in a^2, that is, the fractional error in $N^{\frac{1}{2}}$ is one-half the fractional error in N.

Thus if we write $$N = N_0(1 + f)$$

we must have $$N^{\frac{1}{2}} \simeq N_0^{\frac{1}{2}}(1 + \tfrac{1}{2}f)$$

This follows of course from the result

$$(1 + f)^{\frac{1}{2}} \simeq 1 + \tfrac{1}{2}f$$

which can be established independently.

Again, if $Q = abc$ - - - the fractional error in Q is approximately the sum of the fractional errors in a, b, c, - - - .

In particular, the fractional error in a^n equals approximately n times the fractional error in a. This is true for all values of n, positive or negative.

6. Error in a quotient

If a quantity Q is expressed as the quotient a/b where again a and b have fractional errors f_1 and f_2 respectively, we have

$$Q = a/b$$

$$= \frac{a_0(1 + f_1)}{b_0(1 + f_2)}$$

$$= \frac{a_0}{b_0}(1 + f_1)(1 - f_2 + \text{- - -})$$

$$\simeq \frac{a_0}{b_0}(1 + f_1 - f_2)$$

Thus the fractional error in a/b is approximately the difference of the fractional errors in a and b.

Also if $Q = (abc$ - - -$)/(lmn$ - - -$)$ the fractional error in Q is the sum of the fractional errors in $a, b, c,$ - - - less the sum of the fractional errors in $l, m, n,$ - - - .

EXAMPLE 1

If the current i amperes in a circuit satisfying Ohm's law is calculated from the relation $i = E/R$ where E volts is the e.m.f. in the circuit and R ohms is the resistance, then the fractional error in i due to fractional errors f_E and f_R in E and R respectively is $f_E - f_R$ approximately.

EXAMPLE 2

If g is calculated from the simple pendulum formula $g = 4\pi^2 l/T^2$, and we write $l = l_0(1 + f_1)$, $T = T_0(1 + f_2)$ where f_1, f_2 are the fractional errors in l and T respectively, we have

$$g = \frac{4\pi^2 l_0}{T_0^2} \times \frac{1 + f_1}{(1 + f_2)^2}$$

$$\simeq \frac{4\pi^2 l_0}{T_0^2} \times \frac{1 + f_1}{1 + 2f_2}$$

$$\simeq \frac{4\pi^2 l_0}{T_0^2} \times \frac{(1 + f_1 - 2f_2)}{1}$$

$$\simeq g_0(1 + f_1 - 2f_2).$$

Thus the fractional error in g is $f_1 - 2f_2$. Since f_1 and f_2 may be positive or negative, it follows that the numerical value of the fractional error in g may be as large as $|f_1| + 2|f_2|$ or as small as $|f_1| \sim 2|f_2|$.

If, however, as is often the case in practice, f_1 and f_2 are not known exactly but may have any value between certain limits, the greatest value of the fractional error can be estimated. For instance, suppose f_1 lies between $-F_1$ and $+F_1$, whilst f_2 lies between $-F_2$ and $+F_2$; then $f_1 - 2f_2$ can be as large numerically as $F_1 + 2F_2$. Indeed we can write

$$|f_1 - 2f_2| \leqslant F_1 + 2F_2$$

which gives the greatest fractional error in g.

Instead of this greatest value of the fractional error, a smaller quantity, sometimes called the "most probable" value, is often quoted. It is given by the square root of the sum of the squares of the greatest values of the separate fractional errors, that is, $(F_1^2 + 4F_2^2)^{\frac{1}{2}}$, which clearly is greater than F_1 or $2F_2$, but less than $F_1 + 2F_2$.

7. Use of the calculus

The calculus can be used in the estimation of errors. For suppose x is a measured quantity and y is a quantity calculated from the formula $y = f(x)$. If δx is the error in x the corresponding error in y is δy where

$$\lim_{\delta x \to 0} \frac{\delta y}{\delta x} = \frac{dy}{dx}$$

Therefore $\dfrac{\delta y}{\delta x} \simeq \dfrac{dy}{dx}$ if δx is small enough; that is, the error in y is given approximately by $\dfrac{dy}{dx} \delta x$.

As an example, suppose y is the area of a circle of radius x, so that

$$y = \pi x^2$$

therefore

$$\frac{dy}{dx} = 2\pi x$$

Hence

$$\frac{\delta y}{\delta x} \simeq 2\pi x, \quad \text{if } \delta x \text{ is small}$$

and

$$\delta y \simeq 2\pi x \delta x$$

Thus the error in the calculated value of the area due to a small error δx in the measured value of the radius is $2\pi x \delta x$, and this may be positive or negative depending on the sign of δx. It is, of course, the area of the annulus having radii x and $x + \delta x$.

The fractional error in the area is

$$\frac{\delta y}{y} \simeq \frac{2\pi x \delta x}{\pi x^2} = 2\frac{\delta x}{x}$$

that is, approximately twice the fractional error in the radius, in accordance with the result proved in Section 5.

Of course, most simple examples including that above hardly

need the use of the calculus; a little algebra is all that is necessary as we have shown earlier, but the calculus does facilitate the solution of more complicated problems.

If a quantity Q is a function of several measured quantities $x, y, z, \text{---}$ the error in Q due to errors $\delta x, \delta y, \delta z, \text{---}$ in $x, y, z, \text{---}$ respectively is given by

$$\delta Q \simeq \frac{\partial Q}{\partial x} \delta x + \frac{\partial Q}{\partial y} \delta y + \frac{\partial Q}{\partial z} \delta z + \text{---}$$

The first term $\frac{\partial Q}{\partial x} \delta x$ is the error in Q due to an error δx in x only (that is, corresponding to $\delta y, \delta z, \text{---}$ all being zero), and similarly the second term $\frac{\partial Q}{\partial y} \delta y$ is the error in Q due to an error δy in y only.

This result is often referred to as the **principle of superposition of errors.**

Also, if we suppose that $\delta x, \delta y, \delta z, \text{---}$ can have any value between $-e_1$ and $+e_1$, $-e_2$ and $+e_2$, $-e_3$ and $+e_3, \text{---}$ respectively, then the "most probable" value of δQ is given by

$$(\delta Q)^2 = \left(\frac{\partial Q}{\partial x} \times e_1\right)^2 + \left(\frac{\partial Q}{\partial y} \times e_2\right)^2 + \left(\frac{\partial Q}{\partial z} \times e_3\right)^2 + \text{---}$$

that is, δQ is the square root of the sum of the squares of the greatest errors due to an error in each variable separately.

Taking as an example the simple pendulum formula used earlier we have

$$g = 4\pi^2 l/T^2$$

therefore

$$\delta g \simeq \frac{\partial g}{\partial l} \delta l + \frac{\partial g}{\partial T} \delta T$$

$$\simeq \frac{4\pi^2}{T^2} \delta l - \frac{8\pi^2 l}{T^3} \delta T$$

and

$$\frac{\delta g}{g} \simeq \frac{\delta l}{l} - 2\frac{\delta T}{T}$$

that is $f_1 - 2f_2$, as we found in Section 6. This result is obtained more simply by taking logarithms first, so that

$$\log g = \log 4\pi^2 + \log l - 2 \log T$$

and hence
$$\frac{\delta g}{g} \simeq \frac{\delta l}{l} - 2\frac{\delta T}{T}$$

EXAMPLE 1

A quantity y is expressed in terms of a measured quantity x by the relation $y = 4x - (2/x)$. What is the percentage error in y corresponding to an error of 1% in x?

We have
$$dy/dx = 4 + (2/x^2)$$

so that
$$\delta y \simeq [4 + (2/x^2)]\delta x$$

Percentage error in $y = (\delta y/y)100$

$$\simeq \frac{100}{4x - (2/x)}[4 + (2/x^2)]\delta x$$

$$\simeq \frac{100(4x^2 + 2)}{x(4x^2 - 2)}\delta x$$

Thus if $\delta x/x = 1/100$, the percentage error in y is $(4x^2 + 2)/(4x^2 - 2)$.

It might be noted that this percentage error varies with x and is approximately 1% when x is large. Further, it is obviously large when $4x^2 - 2$ is small, that is, when x lies near to $\pm2^{-\frac{1}{2}}$; this is not surprising since $y = 0$ when $x = \pm2^{-\frac{1}{2}}$. Actually using $\delta y \simeq [4 + (2/x^2)]\delta x$, we find that when $x = \pm 2^{-\frac{1}{2}}$, $\delta y \simeq 8\delta x$.

EXAMPLE 2

A quantity y is calculated from the formula $y = Cx/(1 + x^2)$. If the error in measuring x is e units, find the corresponding error in y and show that for all values of x it does not exceed Ce units.

Now
$$\frac{dy}{dx} = C\frac{1 + x^2 - x(2x)}{(1 + x^2)^2} = C\frac{1 - x^2}{(1 + x^2)^2}$$

therefore
$$\delta y \simeq C\frac{1 - x^2}{(1 + x^2)^2}\delta x$$

If the error δx in x is e unit, the error in y is

$$\delta y \simeq C\frac{1 - x^2}{(1 + x^2)^2}e$$

This can be written $\delta y \simeq CeE$

where
$$E = \frac{1 - x^2}{(1 + x^2)^2}$$

How does E vary with x? When $x = 0$, $E = 1$; when $x = 1$, $E = 0$, and when $x > 1$, $E < 0$. Also $E \to 0$ as $x \to \infty$. Further, E does not change in value when x is replaced by $-x$ and hence its graph is symmetrical about the axis of E and must have the form shown in Fig. 2.

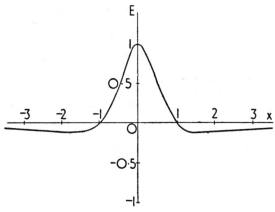

Fig. 2.   Graph of $E = (1 - x^2)/(1 + x^2)^2$

E has a maximum value when $x = 0$ and minimum values when $x = \pm 3^{\frac{1}{2}}$. Thus E lies between 1 (when $x = 0$) and $-\frac{1}{8}$ (when $x = \pm 3^{\frac{1}{2}}$). Hence the error in y lies between Ce and $-Ce/8$.

EXAMPLE 3

The viscosity of water, η, is calculated using Poiseuille's formula giving the quantity of water Q flowing through a cylindrical tube of length l and radius a in time t under a pressure difference p. Find the error in η due to errors in the measured quantities Q, l, a and p.

We have

$$\eta = \frac{\pi p a^4 t}{8lQ}$$

therefore

$$\log \eta = \log (\pi/8) + \log p + 4 \log a + \log t - \log l - \log Q$$

$$\frac{\delta \eta}{\eta} = \frac{\delta p}{p} + \frac{4 \delta a}{a} + \frac{\delta t}{t} - \frac{\delta l}{l} - \frac{\delta Q}{Q}$$

Thus the fractional error in η equals a combination of the fractional errors in p, a, t, l and Q. The term $4\delta a/a$ is usually the most important since a is very small and hence for an accurate determination of η special attention must be paid to the accuracy of measurement of the radius a. Indeed to ensure an accuracy of 1% in η, the radius must be measured with an accuracy of at least 1 in 400.

8. Error in a sum or difference

If a quantity Q is expressed as the sum of two quantities a and b, having errors e_1 and e_2 we have

$$Q = a + b$$
$$= a_0 + b_0 + e_1 + e_2$$

So writing the error in Q as e and the fractional error in Q as f we have

$$e = e_1 + e_2$$

and

$$f = \frac{e_1 + e_2}{a_0 + b_0} = \frac{a_0 f_1 + b_0 f_2}{a_0 + b_0}$$

where f_1 and f_2 are the fractional errors in a and b respectively.

If e_1 and e_2 are known, e and f can be calculated, but as we have noted earlier all that is usually known is that e_1 may have any value between $-E_1$ and $+E_1$ say, whilst e_2 may have any value between $-E_2$ and $+E_2$. What then are the limits between which e and f may lie?

Clearly e can have any value between $-(E_1 + E_2)$ and $+(E_1 + E_2)$, or $|e|$ lies between 0 and $E_1 + E_2$. It is usual to take the "most probable" value of $|e|$ as $(E_1^2 + E_2^2)^{\frac{1}{2}}$ (see Section 6), which is less than $E_1 + E_2$ but bigger than either E_1 or E_2.

On the other hand the fractional error f depends on the values of a_0 and b_0 as well as on f_1 and f_2, and varies between wide limits.

Writing $\quad f = f_1 + \dfrac{b_0}{a_0 + b_0}(f_2 - f_1) = f_2 + \dfrac{a_0}{a_0 + b_0}(f_1 - f_2)$

it follows that if a_0 is numerically much bigger than b_0 then f equals f_1 approximately, or if a_0 is numerically much smaller than b_0 then f equals f_2 approximately. Again if a_0 and b_0 are approximately equal *and of the same sign* f is approximately $\frac{1}{2}(f_1 + f_2)$, whereas if a_0 and b_0 are approximately equal but *of opposite sign* (so that $a_0 + b_0$ is small) f may be large; indeed in general it will be large unless it should happen that $f_1 - f_2$ is very small.

Again the "most probable" value of $|f|$ may be taken to be

$$\frac{\sqrt{(E_1^2 + E_2^2)}}{|a_0 + b_0|}.$$

EXAMPLE 1

If two lengths of l_1 and l_2 are measured as 10.0 and 9.0 with possible errors of 0.1 in each case find (i) the greatest error and (ii) the greatest fractional error in the values of $l_1 + l_2$ and $l_1 - l_2$.

We can write

$$l_1 + l_2 = (10.0 \pm 0.1) + (9.0 \pm 0.1)$$
$$= 19.0 \pm 0.2$$

The greatest error in $l_1 + l_2$ is 0.2 and the greatest fractional error is $0.2/19.0 = 0.01$. Also, $l_1 - l_2 = 1.0 \pm 0.2$ so that the greatest error in $l_1 - l_2$ is 0.2 and the greatest fractional error is as high as $0.2/1.0 = 0.2$. We note that the "most probable" fractional error in $l_1 - l_2$ is $\sqrt{[(0.1)^2 + (0.1)^2]}/1.0 = 0.14$.

EXAMPLE 2

The viscosity η of a liquid is measured by a rotation viscometer. The cylinders are of radii a and b, and a torque G is applied to the rotating cylinder so that

$$\eta = \frac{G}{4\pi\Omega}\left(\frac{1}{a^2} - \frac{1}{b^2}\right)$$

where Ω is the angular velocity of rotation. Calculate the fractional error in η given that $a = 0.04$ m, $b = 0.05$ m, that the greatest error in measuring both a and b is 0.0001 m and that the error in G/Ω may be neglected.

Now,
$$\delta\eta = \frac{G}{4\pi\Omega}\left(-\frac{2}{a^3}\delta a + \frac{2}{b^3}\delta b\right)$$

so that writing $\delta a/a = f_1$ and $\delta b/b = f_2$ we have

$$\frac{\delta\eta}{\eta} = \left(-\frac{2}{a^2}f_1 + \frac{2}{b^2}f_2\right) \Big/ \left(\frac{1}{a^2} - \frac{1}{b^2}\right)$$

$$= 2(a^2 f_2 - b^2 f_1)/(b^2 - a^2)$$

Hence in this case $\quad \delta\eta/\eta = 2(16f_2 - 25f_1)/9$

where the greatest values of f_1 and f_2 are $0.01/4$ and $0.01/5$ respectively.

Hence $|\delta\eta/\eta|$ may be large as

$$\frac{2}{9}\left(16 \times \frac{0.01}{5} + 25 \times \frac{0.01}{4}\right)$$

that is, 0.021 or about 2%.

The "most probable" value of $\delta\eta/\eta$ may be taken as

$$\frac{2}{9}\sqrt{[(16F_2)^2 + (25F_1)^2]} = \frac{2}{9}(0.07) = 0.016$$

If there were also errors in G and Ω the fractional error in G/Ω would have to be added to the value of $|\delta\eta/\eta|$ calculated above.

EXAMPLE 3

In Heyl's method the gravitational constant G is calculated from the formula

$$G = \frac{4\pi^2 I}{A_1 - A_2}\left(\frac{1}{T_1^2} - \frac{1}{T_2^2}\right)$$

where T_1 and T_2 are times of oscillation, I is the moment of inertia of the system about the axis of suspension and A_1, A_2 are constants.

Estimate the fractional error in G due to errors in T_1 and T_2 of $0 \cdot 1$ s when $T_1 = 1750$ s and $T_2 = 2000$ s.

Now since $\qquad G = \dfrac{4\pi^2 I}{A_1 - A_2} \times \dfrac{(T_2 - T_1)(T_2 + T_1)}{T_1^2 T_2^2}$

using the method of Section 7

$$\frac{\delta G}{G} = \frac{\delta(T_2 - T_1)}{T_2 - T_1} + \frac{\delta(T_2 + T_1)}{T_2 + T_1} - \frac{2\delta T_1}{T_1} - \frac{2\delta T_2}{T_2}$$

The first term on the right-hand side may be as large as $\dfrac{2}{10}\left(\dfrac{1}{250}\right)$ and is the most important term. Putting $\delta T_2 = -\,\delta T_1 = 1/10$ we get the largest value of $\delta G/G$ is

$$\frac{2}{10}\left(\frac{1}{250} + \frac{1}{1750} - \frac{1}{2000}\right) \simeq \frac{1}{1200}$$

The values of T_1 and T_2 quoted above are those given by Heyl[2] but the values of δT_1 and δT_2 are hypothetical. Heyl did not give an estimate of the error in the value of G, but it is interesting to note that the value of G he adopted as a result of experiments with gold, platinum and glass spheres was $6 \cdot 670 \times 10^{-8} \text{ cm}^3 \text{ g.}^2 \text{ s}^{-2}$ "with a precision, as measured by the average departure from the mean, of $0 \cdot 005$."

EXERCISES 1

1. If $y = x^2/(1 + x^2)$ find $\delta y/y$ when (a) $x = 3$, $\delta x = 0 \cdot 1$ and (b) $x = 2$, $\delta x = 0 \cdot 05$.

2. If $y = \sin(2\omega t + \alpha)$ find the fractional error in y due to an error of $0 \cdot 1\%$ in t when (i) $t = \pi/2\omega$, (ii) $t = \pi/\omega$. Find also the values of t for which the fractional error in y is least.

3. Find the fractional error in e^x corresponding to an error δx in x. If $x = 0 \cdot 012$ is correct to two significant figures show that e^x may be calculated for this value of x correct to four significant figures.

4. The mass m grammes of an electron moving with velocity v m s^{-1} is $m_0/\sqrt{[1 - (v^2/c^2)]}$ where c m s^{-1} is the velocity of light. Show that the fractional error in m is approximately v^2/c^2 times the fractional error in v, if v/c is small compared with unity.

5. If $i = k \tan \theta$ find the value of θ for which (i) the error in i is least, and (ii) the fractional error in i is least, for a given error e in measuring θ.

6. Given $T^2 = h + (100/h)$ find the value of h for which the error in T is least if the error in h is a constant e. Find also the value of h for which the fractional error in T is least.

7. The diameter of a capillary tube is found by weighing and measuring the length of a thread of mercury inserted into the tube. Estimate the error in the calculated diameter of the tube in terms of the errors in the length, mass and density of the mercury thread.

8. Using Kater's pendulum g is given by

$$g = 4\pi^2(h_1 + h_2)/T^2$$

The length of $h_1 + h_2$ is measured as $1 \cdot 0423 \pm 0 \cdot 000\,05$ m and the time of oscillation T as $2 \cdot 048 \pm 0 \cdot 0005$ s. Calculate g and the greatest fractional error.

If $h_1 + h_2$ is measured as $1 \cdot 042 \pm 0 \cdot 0005$ m, how accurately must T be measured in order that the error in g may be less than 1 in 1000?

9. The surface tension γ of a liquid of density ρ is found by inserting the liquid into a U-tube of which the two limbs have radii r_1 and r_2 respectively. The difference of height h in the two limbs is measured and γ is calculated from the formula

$$\gamma\left(\frac{1}{r_1} - \frac{1}{r_2}\right) = \frac{1}{2}g\rho h$$

Estimate the fractional error in γ if $h = 1 \cdot 06$ cm, $r_1 = 0 \cdot 07$ cm, $r_2 = 0 \cdot 14$ cm, and the error in each of these measurements is not greater than $0 \cdot 005$ cm.

10. The deflexion d of a beam under certain conditions is given by $d = 4We^3/3\pi Ea^4$. Find (i) the maximum fractional error, (ii) the "most probable" fractional error in the value of Young's modulus E calculated from this formula if the error in d is $\pm 0 \cdot 1\%$, the error in e is $\pm 0 \cdot 05\%$ and the error in a is $\pm 0 \cdot 1\%$.

11. A coil of n turns of radius r carries a current I; the magnetic field at a point on its axis at a distance x from the centre is $H = 2\pi n r^2 I (r^2 + x^2)^{-3/2}$. If the error in measuring x is e, find the corresponding error in the value of the field. If e is a constant find for what value of x the error in H is greatest.

12. A large resistance R is measured by discharging a condenser of capacitance C charged to potential V_0; the time t taken for the potential to fall to V is noted. R is given by $t/C \log (V_0/V)$. Find the fractional error in R due to errors in t, C, V_0 and V.

If V_0 and V are measured by a ballistic galvanometer, then $V_0/V = d_0/d$ where d_0 and d are the corresponding deflexions of the instrument. Assuming the errors in d_0 and d are equal in magnitude, show that the greatest value of the corresponding fractional error in R is $f_0\left(1 + \dfrac{V_0}{V}\right)\Big/\log\dfrac{V_0}{V}$ where f_0 is the fractional error in V_0 Find the value of V_0/V for which this is least.

CHAPTER 2

SOME STATISTICAL IDEAS

"The experimental scientist does not regard statistics as an excuse for doing bad experiments."

L. HOGBEN

9. Frequency distributions

Numerical data, including scientific measurements as well as industrial and social statistics, are often represented graphically to aid their appreciation.

The first step in dealing with such data, if they are sufficiently numerous, is to arrange them in some convenient order; this is often done by grouping them into classes according to their magnitude or according to suitable intervals of a variable on which they depend. For instance, the percentage marks obtained in an examination by a number of students could be grouped by counting the number of students who had marks between 0 and 9, 10 and 19, - - -, 90 and 99, thus dividing them into 10 classes. The data could then be tabulated as shown in Table 1, in which the marks of a sample of 120 students have been used.

The number of data in each class is usually called the **frequency** for that class. Table 1 shows what is called the **frequency distribution.** The pairs of numbers written in the columns headed "class," for example, 0 and 9, 10 and 19 and so on, are usually called the lower and upper **class limits.** The **width** of any class is the difference between the first number specifying that class and the first number specifying the next, that is, 10 for each of the classes shown in Table 1. For some groupings, however, the widths of the classes may be unequal.

Table 1

Class	Frequency	Class	Frequency
0– 9	2	50–59	32
10–19	5	60–69	25
20–29	6	70–79	10
30–39	14	80–89	2
40–49	22	90–99	2

The classification shown in Table 1 obviously helps us to appreciate the distribution of marks amongst the students; we can see at a glance, for instance, how many students have fewer than 40 marks and how many have 70 or more. But a graphical representation can make it possibly even clearer. The data are plotted in Fig. 3, where the marks are represented along the horizontal

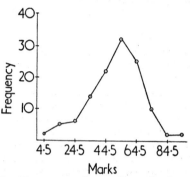

Fig. 3.   Frequency polygon of examination marks.

axis and the frequencies along the vertical axis. The points obtained by plotting the frequency against the mid-value of the corresponding class, namely, $4 \cdot 5$, $14 \cdot 5$, - - -, $94 \cdot 5$ are joined by straight lines and the resulting figure is known as a **frequency polygon**.

A different method is used in Fig. 4 where a series of rectangles

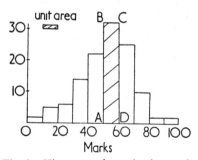

Fig. 4.   Histogram of examination marks.

30

are constructed of width equal to the class width and of area equal to the frequency of the corresponding class, that is, the rectangles in Fig. 4 have areas equal to 2, 5, 6, 14, 22, 32, 25, 10, 2, 2 units respectively. The figure obtained is called a **histogram,** and the total area of the histogram in this case is 120 units equal to the total number of students.

Since the area of each rectangle in a histogram represents the frequency in the corresponding class, the heights of the rectangles are proportional to the frequencies when the classes have equal widths. In this case the mean height of the rectangles is proportional to the mean frequency.

10. The mean

The mean frequency is usually not of particular significance, but what is often important is the **mean** of the data. This is defined as follows: if $f_1, f_2, \cdots f_n$ are the frequencies in the various classes of which $x_1, x_2, \cdots, x_n$ are the mid-values of the variable, the mean value of the variable is given by

$$(f_1 x_1 + f_2 x_2 + \cdots + f_n x_n)/(f_1 + f_2 + \cdots + f_n) \qquad (1)$$

This is the weighted mean of $x_1, x_2, \cdots, x_n$, the weights being the frequencies in the corresponding classes.

It can be written as

$$\sum_{s=1}^{n} f_s x_s / \sum_{s=1}^{n} f_s \quad \text{or} \quad [fx]/[f]$$

and is often denoted by $\bar{x}$.

To evaluate $\bar{x}$ using the expression (1) directly can sometimes be laborious, but the arithmetic can be minimized by using the following simple device.

Let us write $x_s = x'_s + m$ where m is some constant. Then

$$f_1 x_1 + f_2 x_2 + \cdots + f_n x_n$$
$$= f_1(x'_1 + m) + f_2(x'_2 + m) + \cdots + f_n(x'_n + m)$$
$$= f_1 x'_1 + f_2 x'_2 + \cdots + f_n x'_n + m(f_1 + f_2 + \cdots + f_n)$$

31

therefore

$$\frac{f_1x_1 + f_2x_2 + \cdots + f_nx_n}{f_1 + f_2 + \cdots + f_n} = \frac{f_1x_2' + f_2x_1' + \cdots + f_nx_n'}{f_1 + f_2 + \cdots + f_n} + m$$

or
$$\bar{x} = \overline{x'} + m \qquad (2)$$

where $\overline{x'}$ is the mean of the quantities x_s'.

By choosing m conveniently we can make the evaluation of $\overline{x'}$ simpler than the evaluation of $\bar{x}$. It is clear that $\overline{x'}$ will be small if m is chosen near to $\bar{x}$; m is often called the **working** mean or the **assumed** mean.

As a simple example columns one and two of Table 2 give values of x_s and the corresponding values of f_s. In column three are given the values of f_sx_s, so that on addition the mean value of x is given by

$$\bar{x} = \frac{172}{44} = 3\frac{10}{11} \simeq 3 \cdot 9$$

Table 2

x_s	f_s	f_sx_s	$x_s' = x_s - 3 \cdot 5$	f_sx_s'
0·5	1	0·5	−3	− 3
1·5	5	7·5	−2	−10
2·5	7	17·5	−1	− 7
3·5	9	31·5	0	0
4·5	10	45·0	1	10
5·5	8	44·0	2	16
6·5	4	26·0	3	12
sum	44	172·0		18

However, it is simpler to proceed as follows: an examination of the data suggests that the mean is somewhere between $3 \cdot 5$ and $4 \cdot 5$, and so taking $m = 3 \cdot 5$ the values of x_s' are tabulated in column four of the table and the values of f_sx_s' calculated as shown in the last column.

It follows that $\bar{x}' = \dfrac{18}{44}$ and hence

$$\bar{x} = 3 \cdot 5 + \frac{18}{44} = 3\frac{10}{11}$$

as found directly.

It is clear that in this way the amount of arithmetic, and consequently the likelihood of error, is reduced. In many practical cases the economy is considerable.

11. Relative frequency

If the classes specified by $x_1, x_2, - - -, x_n$ occur with frequencies $f_1, f_2, - - -, f_n$, the relative frequency with which x_1 occurs is $f_1/(f_1 + f_2 + - - - + f_n)$, or generally the relative frequency with which x_l occurs is $f_l/\Sigma f_s$. If we denote the relative frequency of x_l by r_l, the mean of the observations can be written as

$$\bar{x} = \sum_{s=1}^{n} r_s x_s$$

We note that r_l is represented in a histogram by the area of the rectangle corresponding to the class of which x_l is the mid-value divided by the total area of the histogram. If the scales are so chosen that the total area is unity then each rectangle represents the corresponding relative frequency.

12. The median

If a set of observations are arranged in ascending or descending order of magnitude the observation in the middle of the set is called the **median**. More precisely, if the number of observations is odd, say $2n + 1$, the median is the $(n + 1)$th value; if the number of observations is even, say $2n$, the middle values of the set are the nth and $(n + 1)$th, the arithmetic mean of which is taken as the median.

For example, the numbers 10, 12, 13, 7, 20, 18, 9, 15, 11 when arranged in ascending order of magnitude are 7, 9, 10, 11, 12, 13, 15, 18, 20 of which the median is 12. If, however, the last value 20 had not been present the middle terms of the set would have been 11 and 12 and the median would have been taken as $11 \cdot 5$.

Sometimes, of course, the data are grouped into classes as for example in Table 1. In this case the total number of students is 120; if the marks were set out in ascending order of magnitude the middle values would be the 60th and the 61st. To find the median we therefore find the marks of the fictitious "individual" number $60 \cdot 5$ in the set. To do this we note that 49 students have marks under 50 and $49 + 32 = 81$ students have marks under 60. Student $60 \cdot 5$ is therefore in the class 50–59, and the median is taken to be

$$50 + \frac{60 \cdot 5 - 49}{32} \times 10$$

that is, $50 + 3 \cdot 6 = 53 \cdot 6$.

13. Frequency curves

It is clear that in general the shape of a histogram depends on the widths of the classes chosen in grouping the data. For instance, when the data used in Table 1 are grouped in classes of half the width the results are as shown in Table 3. The corresponding

Table 3

Class limits	Frequency	Class limits	Frequency
0– 4	1 ⎫ 2	50–54	15 ⎫ 32
5– 9	1 ⎭	55–59	17 ⎭
10–14	2 ⎫ 5	60–64	14 ⎫ 25
15–19	3 ⎭	65–69	11 ⎭
20–24	3 ⎫ 6	70–74	7 ⎫ 10
25–29	3 ⎭	75–79	3 ⎭
30–34	6 ⎫ 14	80–84	1 ⎫ 2
35–39	8 ⎭	85–89	1 ⎭
40–44	12 ⎫ 22	90–94	1 ⎫ 2
45–49	10 ⎭	95–99	1 ⎭

histogram is shown in Fig. 5 which should be compared with the original histogram shown in Fig. 4.

The area of *ABCDEF* in Fig. 5 is $(15 + 17)$ units, the same as the area of the corresponding rectangle *ABCD* in Fig. 4. This is true for all corresponding portions of the two histograms, so that although they have different shapes they have equal areas. The

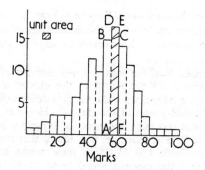

Fig. 5. Histogram of examination marks.

total area equals in each case the total frequency which, of course, is unchanged by any change of class width.

In practice the width of the classes is dictated by the nature of the data, in particular by their number as well as their accuracy; classes either too wide or too narrow do not reveal the general trend of the data. For example, in dealing with the marks shown in Table 1, the smallest possible class width is 1 mark since fractional marks are not given, but in fact a class width of less than 5 marks is probably meaningless as few examiners would claim to be able to mark within 5%. On the other hand the maximum class width is 100, in which case the histogram would consist of a single rectangle from which no useful information could be derived.

Again, if the heights of a group of men were measured to the nearest 0·5 cm, all the men of recorded height 180·5 cm could be put in the class 180·5 and the class-width would be 0·5 cm. This class would include all the men with heights between 180·25 and 180·75 cm, which are known as the **class-boundaries**. On the other hand, using a class-width of 2 cm the class 162–163·5 might include all the men with recorded heights of 162, 162·5, 163, 163·5 cm; strictly in that case it would include all those with heights between 161·75 cm and 163·75 cm, which would be the class-boundaries, and the mid-value of the class would be 162·75 cm. However, in the class 162–164 there might be included the men with recorded heights of 162·5, 163, 163·5 cm and half of those with recorded heights of 162 and 164 cm;

35

the mid-value of the class would then be 163 cm. It is important that there should be no doubt where the boundaries of the classes are, and that there should be no overlap or gaps between successive classes.

It will be noted that the mean of any number of observations depends in general on the width of the classes into which the observations are grouped, since the mean is defined (see Section 10) in terms of the mid-values of the classes. However, provided the class width is not too large the effect of grouping is small and is usually neglected. For example, it is found that the mean of the marks given in Table 1 is $51 \cdot 25$; if these marks are grouped as shown in Table 3 the mean is found to be $51 \cdot 17$. Again, using only one class covering the whole range, 0–99, the mean is $49 \cdot 5$.

With a very large number of data grouped into classes of small width it is clear that the outline of the histogram approximates to a continuous curve, as is illustrated in Fig. 6. Such a curve is known as a **frequency curve.**

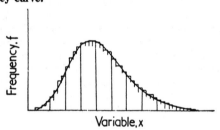

Fig. 6.   Frequency curve.

The area under a frequency curve or under any part of it has special significance. The scales of the frequency curve are often chosen so that the total area under the curve is unity. This total area being finite does not give the total frequency which is infinite, but the area under any part of the curve gives the **relative** frequency for the corresponding range of the variable. The value of the variable for which the ordinate divides the area under the curve into two equal parts is therefore the median. On the other hand the mode corresponds to the maximum value of the frequency.

We shall take some examples of frequency curves later. We merely note here that any finite number of observations might be regarded as a sample taken from an infinite number distributed in a manner indicated by the frequency curve. The histogram of the sample is an approximation to the frequency curve, the degree of approximation depending in general on the number of observations and on the class width. The histogram tends more and more closely to the frequency curve as the number of observations increases and the class width decreases, provided the unit of area is so chosen that the total area under the histogram is always the same as that under the frequency curve, which as stated above is usually taken as unity.

If the equation of the frequency curve is known, that is, f is expressed as some function of the variable x, the mean value of the variable can usually be found by expressing it in terms of integrals, namely,

$$\bar{x} = \int_a^b fx\,dx \Big/ \int_a^b f\,dx$$

where a and b define the range of x. For example, consider the distribution such that the frequency f is given by

$$f = 2/\pi(x^2 + 1)$$

from $x = -1$ to $x = +1$, the factor $2/\pi$ being chosen so that the area under the frequency curve is unity; that is,

$$\int_{-1}^1 f\,dx = \frac{2}{\pi}\int_{-1}^1 \frac{dx}{x^2 + 1} = \frac{2}{\pi}\Big[\tan^{-1} x\Big]_{-1}^1 = 1$$

The mean value of the variable $= \int_{-1}^1 fx\,dx = \frac{1}{\pi}\Big[\log(x^2 + 1)\Big]_{-1}^1$

which is zero. This is obvious from the symmetry of the curve about the axis $x = 0$. The median is also $x = 0$ and so is the mode.

14. Measures of dispersion

A very important characteristic of a set of data is the **dispersion** or **scatter** of the data about some value such as the **mean**.

The numbers 40, 50, 60, 70, 80 of which the mean is 60 have a dispersion or scatter of 20 on each side of the mean; they are all within the limits 60 ± 20. Similarly, the numbers 5, 6, 7, 8, 10, 12 have a mean of 8 and are within the limits $8 - 3$ and $8 + 4$. Different sets of data have, in general, different means and different dispersions. The data corresponding to the frequency curve A in Fig. 7 have a smaller dispersion than those represented by the curve B, whilst the mean of the data A is greater than that of the data B. Various parameters are used to measure the dispersion. We shall mention only three, namely, the **range,** the **mean deviation** and the **standard deviation.**

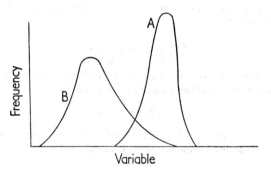

Fig. 7.   Frequency distributions with different means and dispersions.

15. The range

The **range** of a frequency distribution is defined as the difference between the least and greatest values of the variable. This is a very simple measure of dispersion and has, of course, limitations because of its simplicity. It gives the complete interval of the variable over which the data are distributed and so includes those data, usually at the ends of the interval, which occur very infrequently. It may be much more useful in certain cases to know the portion of the range of the variable within which a given fraction, say 50%, of the data lie.

For example the **range** of the marks given in Table 1 is 0–99, but 93/120 or 78% of the marks lie between 30 and 69 inclusive.

38

16. The mean deviation

If $x_1, x_2, \text{- - -} x_n$ are a set of data of which $\bar{x}$ is the mean, the deviations of the data from the mean* are $(x_1 - \bar{x})$, $(x_2 - \bar{x})$, $\text{- - -} (x_n - \bar{x})$ respectively, which we will write as $d_1, d_2, \text{- - -} d_n$. Some of these deviations are positive and some negative; in fact their sum is zero, that is,

$$d_1 + d_2 + \text{- - -} + d_n = x_1 + x_2 + \text{- - -} + x_n - n\bar{x} = 0.$$

The **mean deviation** (sometimes called the **mean absolute deviation**) of a set of data is defined as the mean of the **numerical values** of the deviations.

Therefore the mean deviation is

$$\frac{|d_1| + |d_2| + \text{- - -} + |d_n|}{n} = \frac{1}{n}\sum_{s=1}^{n} |d_s|.$$

For example, the numbers 7, 5, 8, 10, 12, 6 have a mean of 8 and a mean deviation of $(1/6)(1 + 3 + 0 + 2 + 4 + 2) = 2$.

If the data $x_1, x_2, \text{- - -} x_n$ have frequencies $f_1, f_2, \text{- - -} f_n$ respectively, the mean deviation is given by

$$\frac{f_1|d_1| + f_2|d_2| + \text{- - -} + f_n|d_n|}{f_1 + f_2 + \text{- - -} + f_n} = \frac{\Sigma f_s|x_s - \bar{x}|}{\Sigma f_s} \tag{3}$$

EXAMPLE

Consider the data given in Table 2. The mean was found to be $3\frac{10}{11} \simeq 3\cdot9$. In Table 4 below values of $|d_s|$ are given in column three and values of $f_s|d_s|$ in column four, from which it follows that the mean deviation is $\frac{58\cdot0}{44} = 1\cdot32$.

* deviations are sometimes taken from the median.

Table 4

$$\bar{x} = 3{\cdot}9, \quad d_s = x_s - 3{\cdot}9$$

x_s	f_s	$|d_s|$	$f_s|d_s|$
0·5	1	3·4	3·4
1·5	5	2·4	12·0
2·5	7	1·4	9·8
3·5	9	0·4	3·6
4·5	10	0·6	6·0
5·5	4	1·6	12·8
6·5	8	2·6	10·4
sum	44		58·0

17. The standard deviation

The most important measure of dispersion is the **standard deviation,** usually denoted by σ. It is defined in terms of the squares of the deviations from the mean as follows:

If $d_1, d_s, \text{- - -}, d_n$ are the deviations of the data $x_1, x_2, \text{- - -}, x_n$ from the mean $\bar{x}$, then*

$$\sigma^2 = (d_1^2 + d_2^2 + \cdots + d_n^2)/n$$

that is,
$$\sigma = \left[\frac{1}{n} \sum_{s=1}^{n} d_s^2 \right]^{\frac{1}{2}} = \left[\frac{1}{n} \sum_{s=1}^{n} (x_s - \bar{x})^2 \right]^{\frac{1}{2}} \tag{4}$$

If $x_1, x_2, \text{- - -}, x_n$ have frequencies $f_1, f_2, \text{- - -}, f_n$ respectively then

$$\sigma^2 = (f_1 d_1^2 + f_2 d_2^2 + \cdots + f_n d_n^2)/(f_1 + f_2 + \cdots + f_n)$$

$$= \sum_{s=1}^{n} f_s (x_s - \bar{x})^2 \Big/ \sum_{s=1}^{n} f_s.$$

σ^2 is known as the **variance** of the data. The **standard deviation** σ is the **root mean square deviation** of the data, measured from the mean.

If the frequencies f are known for *all* values of x over a continuous

* The reader is asked to note the modification introduced in Section 30.

range (a, b), then the summations can be replaced by integrals and we have

$$\sigma^2 = \int_a^b f(x - \bar{x})^2 dx \Big/ \int_a^b f dx$$

EXAMPLE 1

Find the standard deviation of the numbers 5, 6, 7, 8, 10, 12.

The mean of these numbers is 8, and so the deviations are —3, —2, —1, 0, 2, 4 respectively; the sum of the deviations is, of course, zero.

Now $\sigma^2 = (1/6)(9 + 4 + 1 + 0 + 4 + 16) = 34/6 = 5 \cdot 67$

therefore $\sigma = 2 \cdot 38$.

It might be noted that a **coefficient of variation** is sometimes used. It is defined as $100 \, \sigma/\bar{x}$ and is expressed as a percentage. In the above example the coefficient of variation is therefore

$$100(2 \cdot 38)/8 \simeq 30\%$$

EXAMPLE 2

If the frequency of the variable x is given by $f = Ce^{-x/a}$ for all positive values of x, find the mean and standard deviation of the distribution.

The mean value of x is given by

$$\bar{x} = \int_0^\infty Cx \, e^{-x/a} \, dx \Big/ \int_0^\infty C \, e^{-x/a} \, dx$$

which reduces to $\bar{x} = a$.

Also the standard deviation σ is given by

$$\sigma^2 = \int_0^\infty C(x - a)^2 \, e^{-x/a} \, dx \Big/ \int_0^\infty C \, e^{-x/a} \, dx$$

which reduces to $\sigma = a$.

18. Evaluation of standard deviation, σ

In cases more complicated than the simple example above (Example 1), considerable economy in the arithmetic can be made by using a suitable working mean m, instead of $\bar{x}$.

As shown earlier

$$\Sigma f_s(x_s - m) = \Sigma f_s x_s - m\Sigma f_s$$

so that
$$\frac{\Sigma f_s(x_s - m)}{\Sigma f_s} = \frac{\Sigma f_s x_s}{\Sigma f_s} - m = \bar{x} - m \qquad (5)$$

The summation on the left-hand side, involving deviations from the working mean m, can thus be used to find $\bar{x}$ (see Section 10).

Further,

$$\Sigma f_s(x_s - \bar{x})^2 = \Sigma f_s[(x_s - m) + (m - \bar{x})]^2$$
$$= \Sigma f_s(x_s - m)^2 + 2(m - \bar{x})\Sigma f_s(x_s - m) + (m - \bar{x})^2\Sigma f_s$$

Hence, dividing by Σf_s and using equation (5) above

$$\sigma^2 = \frac{\Sigma f_s(x_s - \bar{x})^2}{\Sigma f_s} = \frac{\Sigma f_s(x_s - m)^2}{\Sigma f_s} + 2(m - \bar{x})(\bar{x} - m) + (m - \bar{x})^2$$
$$= \frac{\Sigma f_s(x_s - m)^2}{\Sigma f_s} - (m - \bar{x})^2$$
$$= \mu^2 - (m - \bar{x})^2 \qquad (6)$$

We note that $\Sigma f_s(x_s - m)^2$ is the sum of the squares of the deviations from the working mean m. It is usually easier, in finding σ^2, to choose a suitable working mean m and calculate $\mu^2 = \Sigma f_s(x_s - m)^2 / \Sigma f_s$ and then use

$$\sigma^2 = \mu^2 - (m - \bar{x})^2$$

The special case when $m = 0$ is of some importance. Also, one further interpretation of equation (6) might well be noted here: *the least value of μ^2 is σ^2 and this arises when $m = \bar{x}$*, that is, the sum of the squares of the deviations of any set of data, measured from any value m, is least when m equals the mean of the data.

EXAMPLE

Calculate the mean and standard deviation of the following observations, where f denotes the frequency of the observation x.

x	0	1	2	3	4	5	6	7	8	9	10
f	10	40	72	85	78	55	32	18	7	2	1

Using a working mean of 3 the necessary working is tabulated below, where d now denotes the deviation from the working mean, that is, $x - m$ with $m = 3$.

The last two columns are calculated for checking purposes as explained later in Section 20.

Table 5

x	f	d	fd	fd^2	$f(d + 1)$	$f(d + 1)^2$
0	10	−3	−30	90	−20	40
1	40	−2	−80	160	−40	40
2	72	−1	−72	72	0	0
3	85	0	0	0	85	85
4	78	1	78	78	156	312
5	55	2	110	220	165	495
6	32	3	96	288	128	512
7	18	4	72	288	90	450
8	7	5	35	175	42	252
9	2	6	12	72	14	98
10	1	7	7	49	8	64
sum	400		228	1492	628	2348

Hence, from equation (5)

$$\bar{x} - 3 = 228/400$$

therefore

$$\bar{x} = 3 \cdot 57$$

Also $\mu_2 = 1492/400$ and hence from equation (6)

$$\sigma^2 = \frac{1492}{400} - (0 \cdot 57)^2 = 3 \cdot 73 - 0 \cdot 32 = 3 \cdot 41$$

therefore $\sigma = 1 \cdot 85$

We note that in this case the coefficient of variation equals

$$(1 \cdot 85/3 \cdot 57) \times 100\% = 52\%$$

19. Sheppard's correction

If we regard the data given in Table 5 as grouped into classes of unit width **Sheppard's correction** should be applied in the evaluation of σ^2. As we have stated earlier (Section 13) the effect of the class width on the mean is usually negligible, but Sheppard has shown that to allow for the class width c the value of μ^2 as calculated above should under certain conditions be reduced by $c^2/12$.

Since $c = 1$ in this case, we have

$$\mu^2 = 3 \cdot 73 - 0 \cdot 08 = 3 \cdot 65$$

and hence

$$\sigma^2 = 3 \cdot 65 - 0 \cdot 32 = 3 \cdot 33$$

therefore

$$\sigma = 1 \cdot 82$$

20. Charlier's checks

As a check on the arithmetic involved in the calculation of $\bar{x}$ and σ we can use the results

$$\Sigma f(d + 1) = \Sigma fd + \Sigma f$$
$$\Sigma f(d + 1)^2 = \Sigma fd^2 + 2\Sigma fd + \Sigma f$$

which are known as **Charlier's checks**.

In the above example $\Sigma f(d + 1)$ and $\Sigma f(d + 1)^2$ have been calculated independently as is shown in the last two columns of Table 5. The calculated values agree with the values obtained using Charlier's checks, for these give

$$\Sigma f(d + 1) = 228 + 400 = 628$$

and

$$\Sigma f(d + 1)^2 = 1492 + 2(228) + 400 = 2348$$

These checks are only partial but are usually worthwhile.

21. The mean and standard deviation of a sum

It is sometimes necessary to find the mean and standard deviation of the sum of two or more sets of quantities, or of two or more functions. It is possible to obtain expressions for the mean and standard deviation of the sum in terms of those of the components forming the sum.

Suppose $x_1, x_2, \text{---} x_n$ and $x_1', x_2', \text{---} x_m'$ are two sets of values of a variable x. Further, suppose the mean values of the two sets are $\bar{x}$ and $\overline{x'}$ respectively. The mean value of the sum or aggregate of the two sets of values is

$$(x_1 + x_2 + \text{---} + x_n + x_1' + x_2' \text{---} + x_m')/(n + m)$$
$$= (n\bar{x} + m\overline{x'})/(n + m)$$

Similarly if σ and σ' are the standard deviations of the two sets of values, the standard deviation of the aggregate of values can be found, by using equation (6) of Section 18, in terms of n, m, $\bar{x}$, $\overline{x'}$, σ and σ'.

Another important example of a sum, however, is where a variable z is expressed as the sum of two or more independent variables x, y, - - -, say $z = x + y$ or more generally $z = ax + by$ where a and b are constants.

Suppose x has the values x_1, x_2, - - - x_n and y has the values y_1, y_2, - - - y_m. Then if $z = ax + by$ it follows that z has the values, mn in number, given by $ax_i + by_j$ with $i = 1, 2, 3, - - - n$ and $j = 1, 2, 3, - - - m$. If the means of z, x, y are denoted by $\bar{z}$, $\bar{x}$, $\bar{y}$ and the standard deviations by σ_z, σ_x, σ_y respectively, it can be shown that

$$\bar{z} = a\bar{x} + b\bar{y}$$

and

$$\sigma_z^2 = a^2\sigma_x^2 + b^2\sigma_y^2$$

In particular if $z = x + y$ we have $\bar{z} = \bar{x} + \bar{y}$ and $\sigma_z^2 = \sigma_x^2 + \sigma_y^2$.

For example, suppose x has the values 10, 11, 12 and y has the values 6, 8, 10 so that $\bar{x} = 11$ and $\bar{y} = 8$, whilst

$$\sigma_x^2 = (1^2 + 0 + 1^2)/3 = 2/3$$

and

$$\sigma_y^2 = (2^2 + 0 + 2^2)/3 = 8/3$$

Then if $z = x + y$, z has the nine values obtained by adding the three values of x to each of the three values of y, namely

	16		18		20	
		17		19		21
			18		20		22

It follows that $\bar{z} = 19$ verifying $\bar{z} = \bar{x} + \bar{y}$.

Also, $\sigma_z^2 = (3^2 + 2^2 + 2 . 1^2 + 0 + 2 . 1^2 + 2^2 + 3^2)/9 = 10/3$ verifying that $\sigma_z^2 = \sigma_x^2 + \sigma_y^2$.

Again, if $z = x - y$ the values of z are

				4	5	6
		2	3	4		
0	1	2				

so that $\bar{z} = 3$ verifying $\bar{z} = \bar{x} - \bar{y}$.

Also, $\sigma_z^2 = (3^2 + 2^2 + 2.1^2 + 0 + 2.1^2 + 2^2 + 3^2)/9 = 10/3$ so that again $\sigma_z^2 = \sigma_x^2 + \sigma_y^2$.

EXERCISES 2

1. Find the mean and the median of the following:
   (a) 10, 12, 14, 16, 17, 19, 20, 21
   (b) the quantities given in (a) when they occur with frequencies 2, 3, 4, 5, 6, 8, 10, 12 respectively.

2. (a) Find the mean deviation of the following:
      15, 21, 19, 20, 18, 17, 22, 23, 16, 25
   (b) Find the mean deviation and the standard deviation of the data given in (a), if their frequencies are respectively:
      1, 11, 12, 14, 9, 6, 9, 5, 3, 1

3. Thirty observations of an angle θ are distributed as follows, f being the frequency of the corresponding value. Calculate the mean and mean deviation of these readings.

θ	f
50° 36′ 20″	1
50° 36′ 21″	2
50° 36′ 23″	4
50° 36′ 24″	6
50° 36′ 25″	8
50° 36′ 26″	5
50° 36′ 27″	3
50° 36′ 28″	1

4. Using (i) 40 and (ii) 50 as the assumed mean find the mean of the variable x which occurs with frequency f as follows:

x	20	30	40	50	60	70	80
f	53	75	95	100	70	35	22

   Find also the median.

5. Find the standard deviation of the distribution given in question 4. Apply Charlier's checks and Sheppard's correction for grouping.

6. Find the mean value of the data given (a) in Table 1, (b) in Table 3.

7. Observations on the scattering of electrons in G.5 plates led to the following results, which give the relative intensity of electrons in tracks of given radii of curvature. Find the mean radius of curvature of the tracks.

Radius of curvature (cm)	5·4	5·5	5·6	5·7	5·8	5·9	6·0
Relative intensity	0	11	36·5	40·5	31	9·5	0

8. Draw the frequency curve (the triangular distribution) given by $f = x$ from $x = 0$ to $x = 1$ and $f = 2 - x$ from $x = 1$ to $x = 2$. What is the mean value of x?
   Find the median for the range $x = 0$ to $x = 2$, and for the range $x = 0$ to $x = 1$.
   Find also the standard deviation for the range $x = 0$ to $x = 2$.

9. Sketch the frequency curve given by $f = Cx^2(2 - x)$. Choose the constant C so that the area under the curve, for which f and x are both positive, is unity; and find the mean value of x over this range.
   Find also the standard deviation.

10. Find the mean deviation and the standard deviation of the distribution given by $f = \frac{1}{8}\pi \sin \frac{1}{4}\pi x$ from $x = 0$ to $x = 4$.

11. The mean of 100 observations is 2·96 and the standard deviation is 0·12, and the mean of a further 50 observations is 2·93 with a standard deviation of 0·16. Find the mean and standard deviation of the two sets of observations taken together.

12. The mean of 500 observations is 4·12 and the standard deviation is 0·18. One hundred of these observations are found to have a mean of 4·20 and a standard deviation of 0·24. Find the mean and standard deviation of the other 400 observations.

13. Find the mean and standard deviations of each of the following distributions:

x	0	1	2	3	4	5	6	7	8
f	1	3	8	12	20	18	16	8	4

x	2	3	4	5	6	7	8	9	10
f	2	5	12	18	26	20	12	4	1

Deduce the mean and standard deviation of the sum of the two distributions.

14. If n_1 quantities have a mean $\bar{x}$ and standard deviation σ_1 and another n_2 quantities have a mean $\bar{y}$ and standard deviation σ_2,

47

show that the aggregate of $(n_1 + n_2)$ quantities has a variance given by

$$\frac{n_1\sigma_1^2 + n_2\sigma_2^2}{n_1 + n_2} + \frac{n_1 n_2(\bar{x} - \bar{y})^2}{(n_1 + n_2)^2}$$

15. If the variable x has the values 0, 1, 2, 3, 4 and the variable y has the values -3, -1, 1, 3, find from first principles the mean and standard deviations of the function given by (i) $x + y$, (ii) $2x - y$, (iii) $3x + 4y$, and (iv) $3y - 2x$. Verify the general results quoted in Section 21.

22. Certain special frequency distributions

The distributions of industrial and social statistics, of scientific observations and of various games of chance are manifold. However, many of them approach closely to one or other of three specially important types of frequency distribution which can be derived and expressed mathematically using the theory of probability.

These are known as the **binomial, Poisson** and **normal** distributions. There are many others.

23. The binomial distribution

On tossing a coin there are two possibilities; we get either heads or tails. We therefore say that the probability of getting heads on any one toss is $\frac{1}{2}$, as is the probability of getting tails.

If we toss a coin a large number of times, say n, we shall find that the number of times we get tails is $\frac{1}{2}n$ approximately. In one trial of 1000 tosses heads were obtained 490 times and tails 510 times. Of course, if n is small, the number of heads in any one trial may well differ considerably from $\frac{1}{2}n$; indeed there may be no heads at all. For instance, if we toss a coin 10 times, we may find we get heads 3 times. If we toss the coin another 10 times, we may get heads 8 times. The question arises: if we toss a coin n times, what is the probability of getting heads m times? (of course $0 \leqslant m \leqslant n$).

It can be shown that on tossing a coin n times the probabilities of getting heads 0, 1, 2, - - - n times are given by the successive terms in the binomial expansion of $(\frac{1}{2} + \frac{1}{2})^n$. For example, on tossing a coin 10 times the probability of getting heads 3 times is

$$\frac{10 \times 9 \times 8}{1 \times 2 \times 3}\left(\frac{1}{2}\right)^7\left(\frac{1}{2}\right)^3 = \frac{15}{128}$$

which is 1 in 8 roughly.

More generally James Bernoulli (1654–1705) showed that if the probability of a certain event happening is p and the probability that it will not happen is q (so that $p + q = 1$), the probabilities that it will happen on 0, 1, 2, 3, - - - n out of n occasions are given by the successive terms of the binomial expansion of $(q + p)^n$, namely,

$$q^n + nq^{n-1}p + \frac{n(n-1)}{1.2}q^{n-2}p^2 + \cdots + p^n$$

Thus the probabilities of getting heads 0, 1, 2, - - - 10 times on tossing a coin 10 times are given by the successive terms of the expansion of $(\frac{1}{2} + \frac{1}{2})^{10}$, that is,

$$\frac{1}{2^{10}}, \ 10 \times \frac{1}{2^{10}}, \ \frac{10 \times 9}{1 \times 2} \times \frac{1}{2^{10}}, \cdots, \ \frac{1}{2^{10}}$$

$$= \frac{1}{2^{10}}(1, 10, 45, 120, 210, 252, 210, 120, 45, 10, 1)$$

These probabilities are represented diagrammatically in Fig. 8. The sum of the probabilities is, of course, unity.

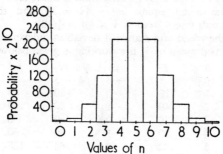

Fig. 8.   Binomial distribution.

A distribution of data having relative frequencies given by the terms of the expansion of $(q + p)^n$ where $p + q = 1$ is known as a **binomial** distribution.

In practice, relative frequencies conforming approximately to these theoretical values are only likely to be obtained if a large number of trials is involved.

It is instructive to represent graphically the frequency distributions corresponding to the terms of the expansion of $(q + p)^n$ for different values of p (and q) and of n. We note that in such distributions the variable n is not continuous; it can only assume positive **integral** values. Further it can be proved that the mean of a binomial distribution is np and the standard deviation is $(npq)^{\frac{1}{2}}$.

EXAMPLE 1

Verify that the data given below, where f denotes the frequency with which an event occurs n times, form a binomial distribution and find the mean and standard deviation.

n	0	1	2	3	4	5
f	1	10	40	80	80	32

Since the first and last terms of the expansion of $(q + p)^n$ are q^n and p^n, if the above are distributed binomially then $(p/q)^5$ must equal 32 or $p/q = 2$, that is, $q = \frac{1}{3}$ and $p = \frac{2}{3}$.

Expanding $(\frac{1}{3} + \frac{2}{3})^5$ we get

$$\frac{1}{3^5}(1 + 10 + 40 + 80 + 80 + 32)$$

which shows that the above distribution is binomial.

Hence the mean equals $np = 5(\frac{2}{3}) = 3\frac{1}{3}$ and the standard deviation equals $(npq)^{\frac{1}{2}} = (5 \times \frac{2}{3} \times \frac{1}{3})^{\frac{1}{2}} = \frac{1}{3}(10)^{\frac{1}{2}}$.

To find the mean and standard deviation independently we can use an assumed mean of 3; the working is given below.

n	f	d	fd	fd^2
0	1	-3	-3	9
1	10	-2	-20	40
2	40	-1	-40	40
3	80	0	0	0
4	80	1	80	80
5	32	2	64	128
sum	243		81	297

Hence the mean $= 3 + \dfrac{81}{243} = 3\frac{1}{3}$ and the standard deviation

$$= \left[\frac{297}{243} - \left(\frac{1}{3}\right)^2\right]^{\frac{1}{2}} = \left(\frac{270}{243}\right)^{\frac{1}{2}} = \frac{1}{3}(10)^{\frac{1}{2}}.$$

EXAMPLE 2

A large batch of articles produced by a certain machine are examined by taking samples of 5 articles. It is found that the numbers of samples containing 0, 1, 2, 3, 4, 5 defective articles are 58, 32, 7, 2, 1, 0 respectively. Show that this distribution is approximately binomial and deduce the percentage of articles in the batch that are defective.

If a large batch of the products contains a fraction p that are defective, the probability of choosing at random a defective article may be taken to be p. Consequently if we choose at random a sample of n articles, the probability that this sample will contain s articles which are defective is given by the $(s + 1)$th term of the expansion of $(q + p)^n$.

The mean of the above distribution is

$$(0 + 32 + 14 + 6 + 4 + 0)/100 = 0 \cdot 56$$

If we equate this to np with $n = 5$ we get $p = 0 \cdot 112$. Taking for simplicity $p = \frac{1}{9}$ the expansion of $(q + p)^n$ in this case is

$$(\tfrac{8}{9} + \tfrac{1}{9})^5 = 9^{-5}(8^5 + 5 \times 8^4 + 10 \times 8^3 + 10 \times 8^2 + 5 \times 8 + 1)$$

$$= \frac{32\,768 + 20\,480 + 5120 + 640 + 40 + 1}{59\,049}$$

$$= 0 \cdot 5549 + 0 \cdot 3468 + 0 \cdot 0867 + 0 \cdot 0108 + 0 \cdot 0007 + 0 \cdot 0000.$$

Hence we should expect the 100 samples to be distributed as follows: 55, 35, 9, 1, 0, 0, which agree well with the numbers actually found.

The distribution is therefore approximately binomial and the percentage of defectives in the batch is likely to be about 11%.

24. The Poisson distribution

The form of the binomial distribution varies considerably depending upon the values of p and n. One important practical case is when p is very small, that is, the probability of the event happening is very small, but n is large, so large that np is not insignificant.

It can be shown that if p is small whilst n is large and such that $np = m$, the binomial expansion of $(q + p)^n$ approximates closely to the series

$$e^{-m}\left(1 + \frac{m}{1} + \frac{m^2}{1 \times 2} + \frac{m^3}{1 \times 2 \times 3} + \cdots + \frac{m^n}{n!}\right)$$

where $e = 2 \cdot 718\,28$ correct to 5 decimal places. This is known as the **Poisson series,** and any distribution which corresponds to the successive terms of this series is called a **Poisson distribution.** It is so named after the French mathematician Poisson (1781–1840), who in 1837 developed the theory.

What characterizes a distribution of the Poisson type is that the relative frequency r with which an event happens n times varies according to the following table:

n	0	1	2	3	- - -	s
$e^m r$	1	m	$m^2/1 \times 2$	$m^3/1 \times 2 \times 3$	- - -	$m^s/s!$

For a true probability distribution the sum of the probabilities must be unity. For a Poisson distribution the sum of the relative frequencies is

$$e^{-m}\left(1 + \frac{m}{1} + \frac{m^2}{1 \times 2} + \cdots + \frac{m^s}{s!}\right)$$
$$= e^{-m} \times e^{+m} \text{ (approximately if } s \text{ is large enough)}$$
$$= 1 \text{ (approximately).}$$

To the same degree of approximation it can be shown that the mean of the distribution is m and the standard deviation is $m^{\frac{1}{2}}$.

In Fig. 9 are drawn histograms of Poisson distributions corresponding to (a) $m = 1$ and (b) $m = 4$.

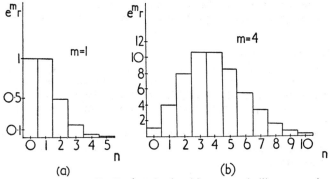

Fig. 9.   Poisson distributions having (a) mean = 1, (b) mean = 4.

Data conforming approximately to Poisson distributions occur widely in science, particularly in biology. They also arise in many industrial problems. The indispensable conditions are that the event should happen rarely (p small) and that the number of trials should be large, or strictly so large that the mean number of occurrences is appreciable.

EXAMPLE 1

The following table gives the frequencies f of the number n of successes in a set of 500 trials. Find the mean of the distribution and verify that the distribution is roughly of the Poisson type. Verify also that the variance equals the mean approximately.

n	0	1	2	3	4	5	6	7	8	9	sum
f	24	77	110	112	84	50	24	12	5	2	500
nf	0	77	220	336	336	250	144	84	40	18	1505

The mean of the number of successes may be found by calculating the values of nf as shown in the table, whence the mean equals $1505/500 = 3 \cdot 01$.

The terms of a Poisson series with this value of m are

$$e^{-3 \cdot 01}(1 + 3 \cdot 01 + 3 \cdot 01^2/2 + 3 \cdot 01^3/6 + \text{- - -})$$

On multiplying by 500 the successive terms become $24 \cdot 6$, $74 \cdot 2$, $111 \cdot 6$, $112 \cdot 0$, $84 \cdot 3$, $50 \cdot 8$, $25 \cdot 4$, $11 \cdot 0$, $4 \cdot 0$, $1 \cdot 4$ which agree very well with the values of f given in the table above.

The variance is found to be $3 \cdot 05$. The working, using an assumed mean of 3, is given below, where $d = n - 3$.

n	d	fd	fd^2
0	—3	— 72	216
1	—2	—154	308
2	—1	—110	110
3	0	0	0
4	1	84	84
5	2	100	200
6	3	72	216
7	4	48	192
8	5	25	125
9	6	12	72
	sum	5	1523

$$\text{Hence, mean} = 3 + \frac{5}{500} = 3 \cdot 01$$

$$\text{and variance} = \frac{1523}{500} - (0 \cdot 01)^2$$

$$= 3 \cdot 0459$$

$$\simeq 3 \cdot 05$$

EXAMPLE 2

The number of dust nuclei in a small sample of air can be estimated by using a dust counter. The following values were found in a set of 400 samples.

Number of particles	0	1	2	3	4	5	6	7	8
Frequency	23	56	88	95	73	40	17	5	3

The mean number of particles is found to be $1170/400 \simeq 2 \cdot 9$. The terms of the Poisson series with $m = 2 \cdot 9$ are

$$e^{-2 \cdot 9} (1 + 2 \cdot 9 + 2 \cdot 9^2/2 + 2 \cdot 9^3/6 + \text{- - -})$$

that is, $0 \cdot 055 + 0 \cdot 160 + 0 \cdot 231 + 0 \cdot 224 + 0 \cdot 163 + 0 \cdot 094$
$+ 0 \cdot 046 + 0 \cdot 019 + 0 \cdot 007 + \text{- - -}$

On multiplying by 400 the successive terms become 22, 64, 92, 90, 65, 38, 18, 8, 3, which agree well with the values of the frequency given above. The degree of departure from the Poisson distribution has been discussed by Scrase.[3]

It might be noted concerning these measurements that the number of dust nuclei in the air is large, and the probability of any one nucleus being within the small sample examined is very small.

EXAMPLE 3

A large batch of articles produced by a certain machine are examined by taking samples of 5 articles. It is found that the numbers of samples containing 0, 1, 2, 3, 4, 5 defective articles are 58, 32, 7, 2, 1, 0 respectively. Show that this is approximately a Poisson distribution (see Example 2, Section 23).

The mean number of defective articles is $0 \cdot 556 \simeq 5/9$ and the terms of the Poisson series with $m = 5/9$ are

$$e^{-5/9} \left(1 + \frac{5}{9} + \frac{25}{162} + \frac{125}{2187} + \frac{625}{26\,244} + \text{- - -} \right)$$

that is, $0·574 + 0·319 + 0·089 + 0·016 + 0·002 + - - -.$ On multiplying by 100 the successive terms become 57, 32, 9, 2, 0, 0, which agree well with the actual values.

25. The normal distribution

The normal distribution was first derived by Demoivre in 1733 when dealing with problems associated with the tossing of coins. It was also obtained independently by Laplace and Gauss later. It is therefore sometimes referred to as the **Gaussian** distribution or the **Gaussian law of errors,** because of its early application to the distribution of accidental errors in astronomical and other scientific data. Its basic importance in physics and statistics cannot be overemphasized.*

The equation of what is known as the normal error curve is of the form $y = A \, e^{-h^2(x-m)^2}$ where A, h, m are constants.

The shape of the curve is shown in Fig. 10. There is a maximum value when $x = m$ and the curve is symmetrical about the line $x = m$.

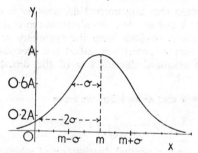

Fig. 10. Normal error curve.
$$y = A \, e^{-h^2(x-m)^2} \quad \text{and} \quad h^2 = 1/2\sigma^2.$$

When $x = m$, $y = A$ and when $x = m \pm a/h$, $y = A \, e^{-a^2}$ which is as small as $A/100$ when $a = 2·15$ approximately.

The whole area under the curve is given by

$$\int_{-\infty}^{\infty} A \, e^{-h^2(x-m)^2} \, dx$$

* "The rôle of the normal distribution in statistics is not unlike that of the straight line in geometry."[4]

and this equals $(A\sqrt{\pi})/h$. If A is taken equal to $h/\sqrt{\pi}$ the area under the curve is unity and the equation of the curve then is

$$y = \frac{h}{\sqrt{\pi}}\, e^{-h^2(x-m)^2} \qquad (7)$$

This is the frequency curve of what is called a **normal** or **Gaussian** distribution. Strictly, such a distribution is one for which the relative frequency of the observations having a value between x and $x + \delta x$ is $y\delta x$ where y is given by equation (7). Another way of expressing this is to say that for a normal distribution the probability that an observation will lie between x and $x + \delta x$ is

$$\frac{h}{\sqrt{\pi}}\, e^{-h^2(x-m)^2}\, \delta x$$

The value of y above, equation (7), is therefore sometimes called the **probability density** or the **relative frequency density** of the distribution.

It will be noted that any normal distribution is determined by two parameters h and m. We can show that m is the mean of the distribution (this is obvious from the symmetry of the curve in Fig. 10) and that h, sometimes called the **precision constant**, is related to the standard deviation σ of the distribution by the relation $2\sigma^2 h^2 = 1$.

Writing $m = \bar{x}$ and $h^2 = 1/2\sigma^2$ we have

$$y = \frac{1}{\sigma\sqrt{(2\pi)}}\, e^{-(x-\bar{x})^2/2\sigma^2}$$

This then represents a normal distribution of which the mean is $\bar{x}$ and the standard deviation is σ. The shape of the curve for the same value of $\bar{x}$ and for different values of σ is shown in Fig. 11.

When $x = \bar{x} \pm \sigma$ we have

$$y = \frac{1}{\sigma\sqrt{(2\pi)}}\, e^{-\frac{1}{2}} \simeq \frac{0\cdot607}{\sigma\sqrt{(2\pi)}}$$

whilst when $x = \bar{x} \pm 2\sigma$ we have

$$y = \frac{1}{\sigma\sqrt{(2\pi)}}\, e^{-2} \simeq \frac{0\cdot135}{\sigma\sqrt{(2\pi)}}$$

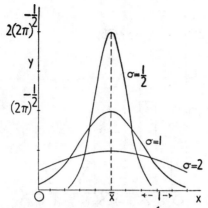

Fig. 11. Normal error curves $y = \dfrac{1}{\sigma\sqrt{(2\pi)}}\, e^{-(x-\bar{x})^2/2\sigma^2}$

26. Relation between a normal and a binomial distribution

It can be verified that the histogram of a binomial distribution corresponding to $(q + p)^n$ approximates very closely, when n is large, to a normal error curve. Indeed the normal distribution can be derived mathematically from the binomial. If the terms of the expansion of $(q + p)^n$ are plotted as ordinates against integral values of x from 0 to n the points are found to lie approximately, if n is large enough, on the normal curve

$$y = \frac{1}{\sigma\sqrt{(2\pi)}}\, e^{-(x-m)^2/2\sigma^2}$$

with m equal to the mean np of the binomial distribution, and σ^2 equal to the variance npq.

In Fig. 12 are drawn the histogram corresponding to $(\tfrac{2}{3} + \tfrac{1}{3})^{10}$, and the normal curve with $m = 10/3$ and $\sigma^2 = 20/9$.

Of course there is one very important difference between the two distributions. The binomial is discontinuous consisting of a set of discrete values corresponding to integral values of n, whereas the normal distribution is continuous extending over all values of the variable. A distribution of discrete values may, of course, approximate closely to a normal distribution.

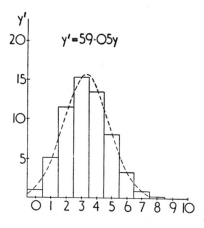

Fig. 12. Histogram of binomial distribution given by $\left(\frac{2}{3} + \frac{1}{3}\right)^{10}$, and (dotted curve) the normal error curve $y = \dfrac{1}{\sigma\sqrt{(2\pi)}} \, e^{-(x-m)^2/2\sigma^2}$ with $m = 10/3$ and $\sigma^2 = 20/9$.

27. The mean deviation of a normal distribution

In Section 16 we defined the mean deviation of any set of data. If we apply this definition to a normal distribution we find that the mean deviation, denoted by η, is given by

$$\eta = \sigma/\sqrt{(\tfrac{1}{2}\pi)} \simeq 0\cdot80\sigma$$

Thus for a normal distribution η equals $4\sigma/5$ approximately. The extent to which any other distribution departs from normality is sometimes estimated by calculating the ratio η/σ and comparing it with 4/5.

For example, if we use the distribution shown in Table 5 (Section 18) we find that $\Sigma f|d| = 592$, whence

$$\eta = 592/400 = 1\cdot48$$

But $\sigma = 1\cdot85$ and hence $\eta/\sigma = 1\cdot48/1\cdot85 = 0\cdot80$.

28. Area under the normal error curve

We have stated earlier that for a normal distribution the probability that an observation will lie between x and $x + \delta x$ is

$$\frac{1}{\sigma\sqrt{(2\pi)}}\,e^{-(x-\bar{x})^2/2\sigma^2}\,\delta x$$

where $\bar{x}$ and σ are the mean and standard deviation respectively of the distribution. This expression is represented by the area under the curve

$$y = \frac{1}{\sigma\sqrt{(2\pi)}}\,e^{-(x-\bar{x})^2/2\sigma^2}$$

between the ordinates x and $x + \delta x$.

Further, the probability that an observation will lie between two values x_1 and x_2 is represented by the area under the curve between the ordinates x_1 and x_2, and equals

$$\frac{1}{\sigma\sqrt{(2\pi)}}\int_{x_1}^{x_2} e^{-(x-\bar{x})^2/2\sigma^2}dx$$

Writing $(x - \bar{x})/\sigma = t$ this expression becomes

$$\frac{1}{\sqrt{(2\pi)}}\int_{t_1}^{t_2} e^{-\frac{1}{2}t^2}\,dt$$

where $t_1 = (x_1 - \bar{x})/\sigma$ and $t_2 = (x_2 - \bar{x})/\sigma$. It can therefore be expressed as the difference of two integrals of the type

$$\frac{1}{\sqrt{(2\pi)}}\int_{0}^{T} e^{-\frac{1}{2}t^2}\,dt$$

This integral has been evaluated for different values of T and is given in mathematical tables.

It might be noted that the function given by

$$\frac{1}{\sqrt{\pi}}\int_{-T}^{T} e^{-t^2}\,dt = \frac{2}{\sqrt{\pi}}\int_{0}^{T} e^{-t^2}\,dt$$

is known as the **error function**, because of its importance in the theory of errors, and is denoted by erf(T).

Hence $\dfrac{1}{\sqrt{(2\pi)}}\displaystyle\int_{0}^{T} e^{-\frac{1}{2}t^2}\,dt = \dfrac{1}{\sqrt{\pi}}\displaystyle\int_{0}^{T\sqrt{2}} e^{-t^2}\,dt = \tfrac{1}{2}\,\text{erf}\,(T\sqrt{2})$

This quantity is represented by the shaded area under the curve

$$y = \frac{1}{\sqrt{(2\pi)}} \, e^{-\frac{1}{2}t^2}$$

shown in Fig. 13.   The total area under this curve is unity.   Also

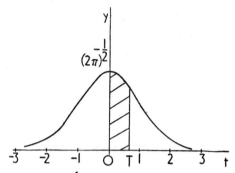

Fig. 13.   Graph of $y = \frac{1}{\sqrt{(2\pi)}} e^{-\frac{1}{2}t^2}$. Shaded area equals $\frac{1}{4}$ if $T = 0 \cdot 6745$.

it can be shown that the area under this curve from $t = -T$ to $t = T$ is $\frac{1}{2}$ if $T = 0 \cdot 6745$.

This last result can be interpreted as follows: in a normal distribution the probability that an observation will lie between $\bar{x} \pm 0 \cdot 6745\sigma$ is $\frac{1}{2}$.   In other words, the quantity $0 \cdot 6745\sigma$ is the deviation from the mean which is just as likely to be exceeded as not, and is sometimes called the **probable error**.   It is not a good term and is falling into disuse.

We give in Table 6 the value of

$$\frac{1}{\sqrt{(2\pi)}} \int_{-T}^{T} e^{-\frac{1}{2}t^2} \, dt$$

for a few important values of T.   From this table it follows that in a normal distribution the probability that an observation lies within 3σ of the mean is $0 \cdot 9973$, that is, the range of a distribution conforming to the normal type is effectively about 6σ. Again, the probability that an observation will lie within the range

60

Table 6

T	erf $(T\sqrt{2})$
0	0
0·6745	0·5
1	0·6827
2	0·9543
3	0·9973
∞	1

$\bar{x} \pm 1·96\sigma$ is 0·95, so this is sometimes called the 95% zone. Similarly the range $\bar{x} \pm 3·09\sigma$ is the 99·8% zone; the probability that an observation will lie *outside* this zone is 1 in 500.

29. Sampling, standard error of the mean

It is usual to regard a finite set of data as a **sample** taken from a much larger, or infinite, set known as the **population**. For example, 100 measurements of a physical quantity, such as a length or a time interval, may be thought of as a sample selected from the very large number of measurements which could be made and which are referred to as the population. The term population is used generally in this way, and not limited to the biological examples to which it was first applied. The importance in statistics of this concept of population cannot be over-emphasized.

Unlike the binomial and Poisson distributions, in which the variable assumes only integral values, the variable in a normal distribution ranges continuously from $-\infty$ to $+\infty$, and an infinite population or number of observations is implied. In practice, however, the number of observations is limited and it is important to know whether such a finite sample approximates to the normal type and, if so, to be able to find the parameters of the normal law which best fit the observations.

A finite number n of observations will conform to a normal distribution if the frequency of the observations that lie between x and $x + \delta x$ is

$$\frac{nh}{\sqrt{\pi}}\,e^{-h^2(x-m)^2}\,\delta x$$

for all values of x. The practical problem is to test this and to find the values of m and h appropriate to the given set of observations. It is clear that a perfect fit is unlikely, but it can be shown that the most probable value of m is the mean of the observations and the most probable value of h^2 is $1/2s^2$ where s is the standard deviation of the observations. We have pointed out earlier that for an infinite population of the normal type $m = \bar{x}$ and $h^2 = 1/2\sigma^2$ where $\bar{x}$ and σ refer to that infinite population.

Of course, if we select at random* a sample of n data from an infinite normal population it is obvious that, in general, the mean of the sample will not be the same as the mean of the whole population; if n is large the two means may not differ very much but if n is small they may. It is possible to express mathematically the manner in which the means of different samples of given size are distributed. In fact it can be shown that this distribution is itself normal and such that its mean equals the true mean of the whole population, whilst its standard deviation equals $\sigma/n^{\frac{1}{2}}$ where n is the number of data in each sample and σ is the standard deviation of the whole population. Fig. 11 illustrates how the distribution of the means of samples retains its normal form but decreases in dispersion as the size of the samples increases. In dealing with any set of data it is therefore usual to find the mean $\bar{x}$ and to write it in the form $\bar{x} \pm \alpha$ where $\alpha = \sigma/n^{\frac{1}{2}}$ and is called the **standard error of the mean.** It should be noted that the quantity $0 \cdot 6745\sigma/\sqrt{n}$ (cf. Section 28) which is called the **probable error of the mean** is sometimes quoted but the use of the standard error is generally recommended and is now widely adopted.

Similarly the standard error of the standard deviation is $\sigma/\sqrt{(2n)}$, so that the standard deviation may be written as

$$\sigma\left[1 \pm \frac{1}{\sqrt{(2n)}}\right] \tag{8}$$

The usefulness and significance of the standard error of the mean may be illustrated by taking a particular example. Suppose the mean of a set of 100 measurements of a certain physical quantity is $2 \cdot 341$ and that the standard deviation is $0 \cdot 18$. Then the standard error of the mean is $0 \cdot 18/100^{\frac{1}{2}} = 0 \cdot 018$, and we write the result as $2 \cdot 341 \pm 0 \cdot 018$. Using Table 6 of Section 28 we infer that if a much larger number of measurements had been made the mean

* **Random sampling** is defined as such that in selecting an individual from a population each individual in the population has the same chance of being chosen.

would be likely to lie between $2 \cdot 341 - 0 \cdot 018$ and $2 \cdot 341 + 0 \cdot 018$ with a probability of $0 \cdot 68$. Further, the probability of the mean lying between $2 \cdot 341 - 0 \cdot 036$ and $2 \cdot 341 + 0 \cdot 036$ is $0 \cdot 95$. These probabilities vary with the value of n and hence it is important to quote the number of observations, especially if it is small, namely,

$$x = 2 \cdot 341 \pm 0 \cdot 018 \text{ (100 observations)}$$

Alternatively, the uncertainty in the value of σ can be indicated by using expression (8) and writing the standard error of the mean as $0 \cdot 018(1 \pm 0 \cdot 07)$.

EXAMPLE 1

The mean height of 200 men is $1 \cdot 705 \pm 0 \cdot 002$ m and the mean height of another 300 men is $1 \cdot 752 \pm 0 \cdot 001$ m. Find the mean height of the 500 men and its standard error.

The mean height of the 500 men is

$$(1 \cdot 705 \times 2 + 1 \cdot 752 \times 3)/5$$
$$1 \cdot 70 + \frac{0 \cdot 01 + 0 \cdot 156}{5} = 1 \cdot 733 \text{ m}$$

Also, the variance of their 500 heights about this new mean may be found by using relation (6) as follows.

Variance of the 200 heights about the new mean
$$= 200(0 \cdot 002)^2 + (0 \cdot 028)^2$$
$$= 0 \cdot 0008 + 0 \cdot 000\ 584 = 0 \cdot 001\ 384$$

Variance of the 300 heights about the new mean
$$= 300(0 \cdot 001)^2 + (0 \cdot 019)^2$$
$$= 0 \cdot 0003 + 0 \cdot 000\ 361 = 0 \cdot 000\ 661$$

$\therefore$ Variance of the 500 heights about the mean
$$= \frac{2}{5} (0 \cdot 001\ 384) + \frac{3}{5} (0 \cdot 000\ 661) = 0 \cdot 000\ 950$$

$\therefore$ Standard error of the mean $= \sqrt{(0 \cdot 000\ 95/500)}$
$$= \sqrt{0 \cdot 000\ 001\ 9} = 0 \cdot 0014$$

$\therefore$ Mean height of the 500 men $= 1 \cdot 733 \pm 0 \cdot 001$ m.

EXAMPLE 2

A set of 400 data has a mean of $2 \cdot 62$. Test whether this can be regarded as a random sample drawn from a normal population with mean $2 \cdot 42$ and standard deviation $1 \cdot 24$.

The standard error of the mean of a random sample of 400 taken from the normal population $= 1 \cdot 24/\sqrt{400} = 0 \cdot 062$.

But the difference between the two means is $0 \cdot 20$ which is more than three times the standard error of the mean. Hence the sample is not likely to be drawn from the given population.

30. Bessel's formulæ

We have not yet discussed how the standard deviation σ of an infinite population can be derived from the standard deviation s of a sample of n data. It can be shown that the best estimate we can make of σ^2 is given by $[n/(n-1)]s^2$. Thus, if the sample is $x_1, x_2, - - -, x_n$ the best estimate of σ^2 is given by

$$\frac{1}{n-1} \sum_{r=1}^{n} (x_r - \bar{x})^2 = \frac{1}{n-1} \sum_{r=1}^{n} d_r^2 \qquad (9)$$

where $\bar{x}$ is the mean of the sample, and $d_r = x_r - \bar{x}$.

This formula differs from that for s^2 in that $(n-1)$ replaces n. This is known as **Bessel's correction.** It is insignificant when n is large.

If the sample consists of the values $x_1, x_2, - - -, x_n$ with frequencies $f_1, f_2, - - -, f_n$ respectively, the best estimate of σ^2 is given by

$$\sum_{r=1}^{n} f_r(x_r - \bar{x})^2 \Big/ (N-1) = \sum_{r=1}^{n} f_r d_r^2 \Big/ (N-1)$$

where $N = \Sigma f_r$ and $\bar{x}$ is the mean of the sample.

Further, it can be shown that the **standard error of the standard deviation** is $\sigma/\sqrt{[2(N-1)]}$. The **standard error of the mean** is, however, $\sigma/\sqrt{N}$.

EXAMPLE

Returning to the data discussed in Section 18, the mean $\bar{x}$ was found to be $3 \cdot 57$. If we apply Bessel's correction the best estimate of σ^2 is given by

$$\sigma^2 = \frac{1492 - 400(0 \cdot 57)^2}{399}$$

$$= \frac{1492 - 130}{399} = \frac{1362}{399} = 3 \cdot 41$$

or $\qquad\qquad \sigma = 1 \cdot 85$

so that, in this case, the correction leaves unchanged the value of σ, correct to two decimal places.

Using Sheppard's correction we get

$$\sigma^2 = 3 \cdot 41 - 0 \cdot 08 = 3 \cdot 33$$

and hence $\sigma = 1 \cdot 82$.

The standard error of the mean is therefore $1 \cdot 82/400^{\frac{1}{2}} = 0 \cdot 091$. The uncertainty in this value is $1/\sqrt{798}$, that is, about $3 \cdot 5\%$, so that the standard error of the mean is $0 \cdot 091(1 \pm 0 \cdot 035)$.

We can write

$$\bar{x} = 3 \cdot 57 \pm 0 \cdot 09$$

31. Peters' formulæ

We have stated earlier in Section 27 that the mean (absolute) deviation, η, of a normal distribution equals $\sigma(2/\pi)^{\frac{1}{2}}$, that is, $4\sigma/5$ approximately.

When we have to deal with a sample of N data drawn from a normal distribution, the mean deviation of the distribution is given by

$$\eta = \sum_{s=1}^{n} f_s|d_s|/\sqrt{[N(N-1)]}$$

where $N = \sum_{s=1}^{n} f_s$. Hence the standard deviation σ of the distribution is estimated by

$$\sigma = \eta\sqrt{(\tfrac{1}{2}\pi)} = \sqrt{\left[\frac{\pi}{2N(N-1)}\right]} \times \Sigma f_s|d_s|$$

$$= 1 \cdot 25\, \Sigma f_s|d_s|/\sqrt{[N(N-1)]}$$

Also the standard error of the mean of the distribution is

$$\frac{\sigma}{N^{\frac{1}{2}}} = \frac{1}{N} \times \sqrt{\left[\frac{\pi}{2(N-1)}\right]} \times \Sigma f_s|d_s| = 1 \cdot 25 \frac{\Sigma f_s|d_s|}{N\sqrt{(N-1)}}$$

These are known as Peters' formulæ. As they involve $|d_s|$ and not d_s^2, they are more readily computed than the formulæ due to Bessel used in the previous paragraph.

If we take the example discussed in Section 18 we have from Table 5 that $\Sigma f_s|d_s| = 592$.

Hence $\sigma = 1 \cdot 25 \times 592/\sqrt{(400 \times 399)} = 1 \cdot 85$ in agreement with the value obtained in Sections 18 and 30.

32. Fitting of a normal curve

It is possible to find the equation of the normal curve

$$y = \frac{N}{\sigma\sqrt{(2\pi)}} e^{-(x-\bar{x})^2/2\sigma^2}$$

which best fits a given frequency distribution by finding the mean $\bar{x}$ and the standard deviation σ of the given distribution in the way explained above. The total area under this curve is N which may be taken equal to the total number of data, that is, the sum of the frequencies.

To test how well the curve fits the data it is useful to calculate the values of $y\delta x$ with δx equal to the width of the classes into which the data are grouped and x equal to the mid-value of each class. These values can then be compared with the given frequencies. We should, as always, not expect reasonable agreement unless the number of observations is large.

As an example let us consider the data discussed above (Sections 18 and 30), of which the mean $\bar{x}$ was found to be $3 \cdot 57$ and the standard deviation σ was $1 \cdot 82$. Since $N = 400$ we calculate

$$\frac{400}{1 \cdot 82\sqrt{(2\pi)}} e^{-(x-3\cdot 57)^2/6\cdot 66}\delta x$$

for $x = 0, 1, 2, 3, - - -, 10$ with $\delta x = 1$.

The values obtained are given as $f(calc.)$ in the following table, which also shows the observed values $f(obs.)$

x	0	1	2	3	4	5	6	7	8	9	10
$f(calc.)$	13	33	60	84	85	65	36	15	5	1	0
$f(obs.)$	10	40	72	85	78	55	32	18	7	2	1

These results are represented graphically in Fig. 14.

The agreement seems reasonably good. It is possible to test "the goodness of fit" by using a special technique, known as the χ^2-test, which enables the significance of the departure of the data from the assumed type of distribution (in the above example, the normal distribution) to be assessed. We cannot go into this here: reference should be made to a text-book of statistics.

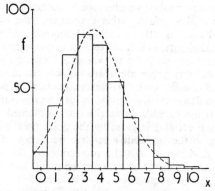

Fig. 14.   Histogram and the corresponding normal curve.

33. Other frequency distributions

Although we have restricted our considerations to the binomial, Poisson and normal distributions it should be emphasized that there are many others. Some of these, such as the **triangular** and the **median** distributions, have been included in the examples. Further, the binomial distribution is a special case of a more general **multinomial distribution** which has many forms. Also the normal distribution which represented by

$$y = A\, e^{-(x-m)^2/2\sigma^2}$$

is such that

$$\frac{1}{y}\frac{dy}{dx} = -\frac{x-m}{\sigma^2}$$

is a special case of more general distributions for which

$$\frac{1}{y}\frac{dy}{dx} = -\frac{x-a}{b_0 + b_1 x + b_2 x^2} \tag{10}$$

These are known as **Pearson's types.**[6]

Many of these other distributions are approximately realized in practice.

It might also be noted here that sometimes what is quite an asymmetrical frequency curve, referred to as **skew,** becomes approximately a normal curve when the frequency is plotted against the logarithm of the variable rather than against the variable itself. Such a distribution is often called a **lognormal** distribution. In plotting such distributions it is convenient to use logarithmic paper, having a logarithmic scale for the variable. Two types of what is known as **probability paper** are also available for plotting normal and lognormal distributions. **Arithmetic** probability paper is such that if the **cumulative** relative frequency of a normal distribution is plotted against the variable a straight line is obtained. Moreover, the mean of the variable is given by the point on the straight line corresponding to the cumulative relative frequency of $0 \cdot 5$, whilst the standard deviation equals the projection on the variable axis of the part of the straight line between the points corresponding to cumulative relative frequencies of $0 \cdot 16$ and $0 \cdot 5$. **Logarithmic** probability paper has, however, a logarithmic scale for the variable, and consequently a lognormal distribution is represented by a straight line.

EXERCISES 3

1. Draw the histograms of the binomial distributions corresponding to $(q + p)^n$ when (a) $q = \frac{2}{3}$, $p = \frac{1}{3}$ and $n = 6$, (b) $q = \frac{3}{4}$, $p = \frac{1}{4}$ and $n = 5$.

2. Calculate from first principles the mean $\bar{x}$ and the standard deviation σ of the two distributions given in question 1. Verify that $\bar{x} = np$ and $\sigma^2 = npq$.

3. Find the frequencies of the Poisson distribution of which the mean is 2. Draw the corresponding histogram. Verify that the variance equals the mean.

4. Show that the following distribution is roughly of the Poisson type, and find its variance.

n	0	1	2	3	4	5
f	21	29	22	12	5	1

5. Write down the binomial distribution corresponding to $(\frac{1}{2} + \frac{1}{2})^{10}$, and fit a normal curve to it. Draw the normal curve and the histogram of the distribution.

6. Make a table of the values of the probability of getting $6 + x$ heads, when 12 coins are tossed, for values of x from 0 to 6.

Show graphically that an equation of the form $y = a\,e^{-bx^2}$ fits these values very closely if a and b are chosen suitably. Find a and b.

7. Fit a normal curve to the following distribution of intelligence quotients (I.Q.).

I.Q. limits	54–	64–	74–	84–	94–	104–	114–	124–	134–144
Frequency	1	2	9	22	33	22	8	2	1

Draw the normal curve and the histogram of the distribution. Find the ratio η/σ for the data.

8. The number of stoppages on 400 consecutive shifts in an industrial undertaking were recorded as follows:

Stoppages per shift	0	1	2	3	4	5
Number of shifts	245	119	30	4	2	0

Show that the distribution is approximately of the Poisson type.

9. Rutherford and Geiger[5] using the scintillation method counted the number of α-particles emitted per unit of time by polonium. Their results are given below; f is the number of times N α-particles were observed. Show that the mean number of α-particles emitted is $3 \cdot 87$ and find the Poisson distribution corresponding to this mean. Compare this with the observed values.

N	0	1	2	3	4	5	6	7	8	9	10	11	12	13	14
f	57	203	383	525	532	408	273	139	45	27	10	4	0	1	1

10. The results of certain measurements on the breakdown voltages of one hundred insulators are given below; n is the number of insulators with a breakdown voltage less than E kV.

Breakdown voltages, E	110	120	130	140	150	160	170	180	190	200	210
Number of insulators, n	0	3	7	15	26	55	78	92	96	99	100

Find the mean and standard deviation, and verify that the distribution is roughly normal. (Check your results by using arithmetic probability paper.)

11. Assuming that the following distribution is approximately normal, find the mean and its standard error. Use (a) Bessel's formulæ, (b) Peters' formulæ.

x	25	26	27	28	29	30	31	32	33	34
f	1	5	17	49	85	52	25	11	4	1

12. If the value of a quantity x and its standard error are given as $10 \cdot 23 \pm 0 \cdot 12$, what is the probability that the accurate value of x will lie between (i) $10 \cdot 11$ and $10 \cdot 35$, (ii) $10 \cdot 11$ and $10 \cdot 47$, (iii) $10 \cdot 11$ and $10 \cdot 31$, and (iv) $10 \cdot 0$ and $10 \cdot 5$.

13. One thousand electric lamps are tested, and it is found that they have an average life of 950 burning hours with a standard deviation of 150 hours. What number of lamps may be expected to have a life of (a) less than 650 hours, (b) between 800 and 1100 hours, and (c) between 1100 and 1250 hours.

14. A sample of 20 data was found to have a mean of $80 \cdot 1$ with standard deviation $2 \cdot 2$. Another sample of 40 had a mean of $81 \cdot 4$ with standard deviation $3 \cdot 4$. Assuming the two samples were taken from the same normal population, use the 60 data to estimate the mean of the population and its standard error.

15. The diameters of the spores of lycopodium can be found by an interference method. The results of an experiment are given below, where $k = 5880$ when the diameters are measured in centimetres.

$k \times diameter$	14	15	16	17	18	19	20	21	22	23
Number of spores	1	1	8	24	48	58	35	16	8	1

Find the mean diameter of the spores and the standard error. Represent the results by a histogram and draw the corresponding normal error curve.

16. Plot the frequency curve for the distribution given by $f = 2/[\pi(x^2 + 1)]$ from $x = -1$ to $x = 1$. Find approximately the standard deviation of this distribution by using the values of x from 0 to 1 at intervals of $0 \cdot 2$.

17. The median law is defined by $f = (1/2a) e^{-|x|/a}$ for all values of x. Sketch the frequency curve and show that the area under it is unity. Find the standard deviation.

18. The results of examining 213 discharge tubes and noting the voltage associated with a particular operating characteristic are given below. Verify that the distribution is approximately normal. Sketch the normal curve and the histogram of the data.

Voltages	97	98	99	100	101	102	103	104	105	106	107	108	109
Number of tubes	1	8	10	25	32	42	42	27	15	4	3	3	1

19. Results of a count of warp breakages during the weaving of particular lengths of cloth are given below. Show that the distribution is approximately Poissonian.

Warp breaks per length of cloth	0	1	2	3	4	5	6
Frequency	15	26	21	19	8	3	0

20. Tests made on electrical contacts to examine how often the contacts failed to interrupt the circuit due to their welding together yielded the following results.

Number of welds per test	0	1	2	3	4	5
Frequency	10	13	13	8	4	2

Show that the distribution is roughly Poissonian, and find its variance.

21. According to the kinetic theory the velocities of the molecules of a gas are such that the component velocities in any one direction are distributed normally (Maxwellian distribution). Thus the probability that a molecule has a velocity-component, measured parallel to the axis of x, lying between u and $u + \delta u$ is $A\,e^{-hmu^2}\delta u$ where A, h and m are constants. Show that $A = (hm/\pi)^{\frac{1}{2}}$, and find the mean value of the velocity-component u.

22. Using the result quoted in question 21, show that the probability that a molecule has a velocity lying between c and $c + \delta c$ where c has components u, v, w parallel to the co-ordinate axes is

$$(hm/\pi)^{3/2}\,e^{-hmc^2}\,\delta u\,\delta v\,\delta w$$

Find the mean value of c and of c^2.

71

CHAPTER 3

THEORY OF ERRORS

"Everybody believes in the exponential law of errors; the experimenters because they think it can be proved by mathematics; and the mathematicians because they believe it has been established by observation."[7]

34. The normal or Gaussian law of error

The function
$$y = \frac{1}{\sigma\sqrt{(2\pi)}}\, e^{-(x-\bar{x})^2/2\sigma^2}$$

which defines a normal frequency distribution is often called the **Gaussian law of error.** This "law" states that measurements of a given quantity which are subject to accidental errors are distributed normally about the mean of the observations. More precisely, the law infers that any set of measurements of a given quantity may be regarded as a sample taken from a very large population—the aggregate of all the observations that could be made if the instruments and time allowed—and that this population is normal.

The two parameters $\bar{x}$ and σ characterizing this normal distribution can be estimated by calculating the mean and standard deviation of the given set of measurements, as explained in Section 30. Indeed, the mean of these measurements is the best estimate of the value of the measured quantity, whilst the standard deviation provides the best estimate of the accuracy so obtained. The value of the measured quantity is usually written as $\bar{x} \pm \alpha$ where $\alpha = \sigma/\sqrt{n}$ is the standard error of the mean and n is the number of measurements. (As we have mentioned earlier some writers use not the standard error but the probable error of the mean which is $0\cdot6745\sigma/\sqrt{n}$, that is, $\frac{2}{3}\alpha$ approximately.)

EXAMPLE

Certain values of the velocity of light obtained using different methods are given below in kilometres per second. Find the mean and its standard error.

Velocity	d	d^2
299 782	2	4
299 798	18	324
299 786	6	36
299 774	− 6	36
299 771	− 9	81
299 776	− 4	16
sum	7	497

A working mean of 299 780 may be used. In the second column of the above table are given the values of the residuals d, relative to the working mean, and in the third column the squares, d^2.

Mean value $= 299\,780 + 7/6 = 299\,781$

further $$\sigma^2 = \frac{497 - 6(7/6)^2}{5} = 98$$

therefore $\sigma = 9 \cdot 9$

standard error of the mean $= 9 \cdot 9/\sqrt{6} = 4$

velocity of light $= 299\,781 \pm 4 \text{ km s}^{-1}$ (6 observations)

As there are only six values the uncertainty in the value of the standard error is considerable, namely, $1/10^{\frac{1}{2}}$, so that the standard error might be written as $4(1 \pm 0 \cdot 32)$.

35. Applicability of the normal law of error

Some groups of observational data in science satisfy closely the normal error law, but it is by no means universally true. Perhaps this is not surprising since any theoretical derivation of the law is based on special assumptions which may or may not correspond to observational conditions.

This so-called Gaussian law of error was first deduced theoretically by Laplace in 1783; he started from the assumptions that the deviation of any one of a set of observations from the mean of the set is the resultant of a large number of very small deviations due to independent causes, and that positive and negative deviations of the same size are equally probable. (Cases can be quoted, however, where a large number of independent causes, each giving rise to a small deviation, do not result in deviations from the mean conforming to the normal law.[8])   Subsequently, Gauss gave a proof based on the postulate that the most probable value of any number of equally good observations is their arithmetic mean.

Both Laplace and Gauss discussed examples of measurements which suggested a wide applicability of the normal law to the distribution of accidental errors and its truth was generally accepted. But more recently its validity has been challenged on various grounds.   In 1901, Karl Pearson showed that some series of measurements which had been deemed to support the normal law showed significant departures from it.   Later, with collaborators, he made six series of observations resembling those of the determination of right ascension and declination using a transit circle, and he found again substantial departures from the normal law.   Jeffreys[9] has re-examined Pearson's data and confirmed the main result; in addition he has shown that the data satisfy a law of Pearson's type VII.

It is now generally agreed that the normal law of error is not universally valid.   Nevertheless it is used widely unless there is evidence to show that some quite different probability distribution applies.   It is worthy of note that even when the parent population is not normally distributed, the distribution of the means of samples of a given size is usually closer to a normal distribution than the population itself.   Jeffreys[6] concludes: "The normal law of error cannot be theoretically proved.   Its justification is that in representing many types of observations it is apparently not far wrong, and is much more convenient to handle than others that might or do represent them better."

Of course the applicability of the normal or any other law can be examined using the χ^2-test but the physicist, unlike the biologist, seldom uses this, perhaps because of the small number of observations with which he usually has to deal.   However, certain large groups of physical measurements do exist and some have been carefully examined.

36. Normal error distributions

A much discussed example of observational data satisfying the normal error law was given originally by Bessel.[10]   He provided the following data concerning the errors involved in measuring the right ascension of stars.   In the first column are given the magnitude of the error of the observation in seconds of time, and in the second column the frequency of its occurrence in a total of 300 determinations. It will be noted that positive and negative errors are grouped together, and so we can only assume they are equally divided. Consequently the mean of the distribution is zero.

Limits of error	Frequency f	fx²	Calculated frequency
0·0–0·1	114	0·285	103
0·1–	84	1·890	85
0·2–	53	3·312	57
0·3–	24	2·940	32
0·4–	14	2·835	15
0·5–	6	1·815	6
0·6–	3	1·268	2
0·7–	1	0·562	0
0·8–	1	0·722	0
0·9–	0	0	0
sum	300	15·629	300

The third column of the table gives the product of the frequency and the square of the deviation x. We measure x from the mean to the mid-point of each class, that is, $0·05, 0·15, - - -, 0·95$.

Hence we have

$$\sigma^2 = 15·629/299 = 0·052\,27$$

Applying Sheppard's correction we get

$$\sigma^2 = 0·052\,27 - (0·1)^2/12 = 0·051\,44$$

or $\sigma = 0·227$

Hence the normal error function corresponding to the data is

$$y = \frac{300}{0·227\sqrt{(2\pi)}}\, e^{-x^2/0·1029}$$
$$= 527\, e^{-9·72x^2}$$

In column four of the table above are given the calculated values of $f = 0·2y$ for the values of x corresponding to the mid-points of each class. The factor 2 is necessary to include negative as well as positive values of x and the factor $0·1$ because of the class width. The normal error curve and the histogram of the data are drawn in Fig. 15.

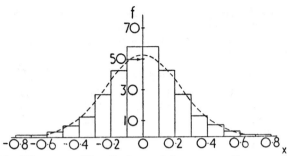

Fig. 15. Histogram of Bessel's data and the corresponding normal curve.

It is clear that the agreement is very good. Hansmann[11] has, however, examined the data and shown that there are two types of Pearson curve that give even a better fit than the normal curve. Jeffreys[9] has also discussed the data and in particular examined how closely they follow the normal error law; he comments: "This agreement is therefore surprisingly good, indeed a little too good, because it suggests that this series has been selected because it gives an unusually good agreement with the law and that others that may have disagreed violently with it may have been suppressed. This danger of selection makes it undesirable to make use of published series to test the law, unless there is some definite reason to believe that no suppression has taken place."

There are other difficulties in attempting to test the law, not least for the physicist that observational data in physics are seldom sufficiently numerous. But even when the number of observations is large they are sometimes invalidated in various ways. For example, Michelson, Pease and Pearson obtained 2885 values of the velocity of light from observations made on about 165 different occasions extending over about two years. The data are symmetrically distributed about the mean value of 299 774 km s^{-1} but the distribution of the residuals is not normal. Birge[12] points out that a very good fit can be obtained if one takes the sum of two normal error curves, with standard deviations of 5 and 15 km s^{-1} respectively, which suggests, as one possibility, two groups of observations of unequal degrees of accuracy. He adds: "The point is that if a large assortment of observations are *not* of equal reliability, their residuals cannot be expected to follow a normal error curve, and I am more and more convinced that the deviations from such a curve found so commonly in large groups of physical measurements are due usually just to this cause." Several attempts to provide suitable measurements have therefore been made. Besides those of Karl Pearson mentioned earlier, Birge[13] made a series of 500 cross-hair settings "on a very wide but symmetrical solar spectrum line, under conditions as favourable as possible to equal reliability for all observations." His results are shown in Fig. 16

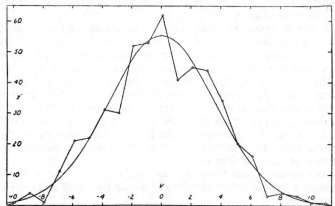

Fig. 16. The distribution of residuals for 500 measurements of a spectral line, compared with the Gaussian error curve evaluated by second moments. Abscissa represents residual v, in 0·001 mm units. Ordinate represents the number of residuals of magnitude v.
(Reproduced from *Physical Review*.)

where the abscissa unit is 0·001 mm and the ordinate y' represents the number of residuals of magnitude v. The smooth curve drawn in Fig. 16 corresponds to the normal error curve

$$y = \frac{h}{\sqrt{\pi}}\, e^{-h^2 x^2}$$

with h, as calculated from the observations, equal to 0·1965 and $y' = 500\, y$. It is clear that over the whole range the observations follow the Gaussian curve very closely.

A similar series of observations, 1026 in number, have been made by Bond who viewed an illuminated slit using a travelling

77

microscope slightly out of focus. The conditions resembled those in the measurement of a spectrum line. Bond's data were originally given as an example of the normal error law, which they seemed to satisfy very well, but Jeffreys[9] subsequently examined them and found systematic departures from the normal law.

37. Standard error of a sum or difference

We discussed in Chapter 1 (Section 7) the resultant error in any quantity which is a function of a number of quantities all subject to experimental error.

It is now necessary to consider the estimation of the standard error of any quantity when the standard errors of the quantities on which it depends are known. For instance, suppose a quantity z is a function of two measured quantities x and y, say, $z = f(x, y)$. If the quantities x are distributed about their mean $\bar{x}$ with a standard error α and the quantities y are distributed about their mean $\bar{y}$ with a standard error β, how are the quantities z, obtained by evaluating $f(x, y)$ for the measured values of x and y, distributed?

To answer this question we use an important property of the normal error law, sometimes referred to as its **reproductive property**. It may be stated as follows:

Any deviation, which can be expressed as the sum of a set of deviations each of which satisfies the normal law, itself satisfies the normal law.

Suppose a deviation D can be written as a linear function of the *independent* deviations $d_1, d_2, \text{ - - - } d_n$ in the form

$$D = k_1 d_1 + k_2 d_2 + \text{ - - - } + k_n d_n$$

where $k_1, k_2, \text{ - - - } k_n$ are constants.

Suppose further that each of the deviations d_s satisfies the normal law so that the probability that d_s lies between x and $x + \delta x$ is given by

$$\frac{1}{\sigma_s \sqrt{(2\pi)}} e^{-x^2/2\sigma_s^2} \delta x$$

Then it can be shown[14] that the probability that D lies between x and $x + \delta x$ is given by

$$\frac{1}{\sigma \sqrt{(2\pi)}} e^{-x^2/2\sigma^2} \delta x$$

where
$$\sigma^2 = k_1^2 \sigma_1^2 + k_2^2 \sigma_2^2 + \text{ - - - } + k_n^2 \sigma_n^2 \tag{11}$$

In other words, D satisfies a normal law determined by the standard deviation σ.

Certain particular cases are specially important.

(i) If $D = d_1 + d_2$ we get

$$\sigma^2 = \sigma_1^2 + \sigma_2^2$$

Also if $D = d_1 - d_2$, then again $\sigma^2 = \sigma_1^2 + \sigma_2^2$. We have verified these results earlier (cf. Section 21) in a few simple cases. We note that σ is greater than either σ_1 or σ_2 but less than $\sigma_1 + \sigma_2$.

More generally, if

$$D = d_1 + d_2 + \cdots + d_n$$

we get

$$\sigma^2 = \sigma_1^2 + \sigma_2^2 + \cdots + \sigma_n^2$$

If $\sigma_1 = \sigma_2 = \cdots = \sigma_n$ then $\sigma = \sigma_1 \sqrt{n}$. But if $d_1 = d_2 = \cdots = d_n$ the deviations are not independent and so the above result does not hold. However, in this case $D = nd_1$ and hence $\sigma = n\sigma_1$.

(ii) If D is the arithmetic mean of $d_1, d_2, \cdots, d_n$ so that $D = (d_1 + d_2 + \cdots + d_n)/n$ we get

$$\sigma^2 = (\sigma_1^2 + \sigma_2^2 + \cdots + \sigma_n^2)/n^2$$

When $\sigma_1 = \sigma_2 = \cdots = \sigma_n$ this reduces to $\sigma^2 = \sigma_1^2/n$ or $\sigma = \sigma_1/\sqrt{n}$, which accounts for the value of the standard error of the mean quoted in Section 29.

(iii) It follows from cases (i) and (ii) that if a set of n_1 data has standard deviation σ_1, and another set of n_2 data has standard deviation σ_2, then the standard error of the sum or difference of the means of the two sets of data is $\left(\dfrac{\sigma_1^2}{n_1} + \dfrac{\sigma_2^2}{n_2}\right)^{\frac{1}{2}}$

It follows that if two quantities are given as $a \pm \alpha$ and $b \pm \beta$ where α and β are the standard errors of a and b respectively, the sum of the two quantities is $a + b \pm \sqrt{(\alpha^2 + \beta^2)}$ and the difference of the two quantities is $a - b \pm \sqrt{(\alpha^2 + \beta^2)}$.

EXAMPLE 1

A sample of 250 observations has a standard deviation of 3 and another sample of 400 observations of the same quantity has a standard deviation of 5. Calculate the standard error of the mean of each sample and the standard error of the difference of the two means.

The standard error of the mean of the first sample is

$$3/\sqrt{250} = 0 \cdot 19$$

The standard error of the mean of the second sample is

$$5/\sqrt{400} = 0 \cdot 25$$

The standard error of the difference of the two means

$$= \sqrt{\left[\left(\frac{3}{\sqrt{250}}\right)^2 + \left(\frac{5}{\sqrt{400}}\right)^2\right]} = \sqrt{\frac{394}{4000}} = 0 \cdot 31$$

Thus if the two means have values m_1 and m_2 the difference of the means can be written as

$$m_1 - m_2 \pm 0 \cdot 31$$

The ratio $|m_1 - m_2|/0 \cdot 31$ is obviously of some practical importance. From Table 6 (Section 28) we note that if $|m_1 - m_2| > 3(0 \cdot 31)$, it may be concluded that the two samples are not likely to belong to the same population; the probability that they so belong is less than $0 \cdot 2 \%$.

EXAMPLE 2

Determinations of e/m for the electron by two different groups of methods give the following results: $1 \cdot 758\,80 \pm 0 \cdot 000\,42$ and $1 \cdot 759\,59 \pm 0 \cdot 000\,36$, the unit being 10^{11} C kg^{-1}. Do the two groups of measurement differ systematically?

The difference between the two mean values is

$$10^{-5}[79 \pm \sqrt{(42^2 + 36^2)}]$$

that is, $0 \cdot 000\,79 \pm 0 \cdot 000\,55$.

Thus the difference of the means is about $1 \cdot 4$ times its standard error, and so the existence of a systematic error is not ruled out.

Birge comments: "In view, however, of the many serious sources of systematic error that have been revealed, from time to time, in almost every method of determining e/m, I think that the small remaining discrepancy should not be taken too seriously."

It might be added here that in trying to assess the significance of the difference of the means of two samples, especially small samples, use may be made of what is usually called the t-distribution.

We have stated earlier (Section 29) that the mean $\bar{x}$ of a sample of n taken from a normal population, of mean m and standard deviation σ, is such that the deviation $\bar{x} - m$ is distributed normally with mean zero and standard deviation $\sigma/\sqrt{n}$. This implies that the ratio $(\bar{x} - m) : \sigma/\sqrt{n}$ is distributed normally about zero with unit standard deviation. However, when the standard deviation σ is estimated from a given sample of n as explained in Section 30, the distribution of the ratio $t = (\bar{x} - m)\sqrt{n}/\sigma$ is not normal, but it has been evaluated and is given in many books[15] on statistics. From the table of t can be obtained, for any value of n, the probability that a value of t will be exceeded in random sampling.

38. Standard error of a product

Suppose $z = xy$ where x and y are measured quantities of which the means are $\bar{x}$ and $\bar{y}$ respectively. Suppose the standard error of $\bar{x}$ is α and of $\bar{y}$ is β.

If we write $x = \bar{x} + x'$ and $y = \bar{y} + y'$ the mean of x' is zero and its standard error is α, whilst the mean of y' is zero and its standard error is β.

We have
$$z = (\bar{x} + x')(\bar{y} + y')$$
$$= \bar{x}\bar{y} + \bar{x}y' + \bar{y}x' + x'y'$$

The mean of z, denoted by $\bar{z}$, is therefore $\bar{x}\bar{y}$. Further, the deviation of z from $\bar{x}\bar{y}$ is $\bar{x}y' + \bar{y}x'$ approximately, and hence using equation (11), Section 37, the standard error of z is γ where

$$\gamma^2 = (\bar{x}\beta)^2 + (\bar{y}\alpha)^2$$

We can write
$$\bar{z} = \bar{x}\bar{y} \pm \gamma$$

and we note that
$$(\gamma/\bar{x}\bar{y})^2 = (\alpha/\bar{x})^2 + (\beta/\bar{y})^2$$

$\alpha/\bar{x}$ is what might be called the fractional standard error of $\bar{x}$, so that the above result indicates that the square of the fractional standard error of the product equals the sum of the squares of the fractional standard errors of the factors forming the product.

For example, suppose the sides of a rectangle are given as $20 \cdot 00 \pm 0 \cdot 04$ cm and $10 \cdot 00 \pm 0 \cdot 03$ cm. The area of the rectangle can be written as $200 \cdot 00 \pm \gamma$ cm^2 where

$$\left(\frac{\gamma}{200}\right)^2 = \left(\frac{0 \cdot 04}{20}\right)^2 + \left(\frac{0 \cdot 03}{10}\right)^2$$

therefore $\qquad \gamma^2 = 0 \cdot 16 + 0 \cdot 36 = 0 \cdot 52$

that is $\qquad \gamma = 0 \cdot 72$

39. Standard error of a compound quantity

Collecting together and extending the results of the previous two paragraphs we have:

If a number of measured quantities have means $m_1, m_2, \text{ - - -}, m_n$ with standard errors $\alpha_1, \alpha_2, \text{ - - -}, \alpha_n$ respectively then the standard error of

   (i) the sum $m_1 + m_2$ is $\sqrt{(\alpha_1^2 + \alpha_2^2)}$

   (ii) the difference $m_1 - m_2$ is $\sqrt{(\alpha_1^2 + \alpha_2^2)}$

   (iii) the multiple km_1 is $k\alpha_1$

   (iv) the product m_1m_2 is $\sqrt{(m_1^2\alpha_2^2 + m_2^2\alpha_1^2)}$

   (v) the product $m_1m_2m_3$ is α where

$$(\alpha/m_1m_2m_3)^2 = (\alpha_1/m_1)^2 + (\alpha_2/m_2)^2 + (\alpha_3/m_3)^2$$

   (vi) the power m_1^p is α where

$$\alpha/m_1^p = p\alpha_1/m_1$$

or $\qquad\qquad\qquad \alpha = (pm_1^{p-1})\alpha_1$

   (vii) any function of $m_1, m_2, \text{ - - -}, m_n$, namely, $f(m_1, m_2, \text{ - - -}, m_n)$, is α where

$$\alpha^2 = \left(\frac{\partial f}{\partial m_1}\right)^2\alpha_1^2 + \left(\frac{\partial f}{\partial m_2}\right)^2\alpha_2^2 + \text{ - - -} + \left(\frac{\partial f}{\partial m_n}\right)^2\alpha_n^2$$

Of course (i) to (vi) are special cases of (vii).

EXAMPLE 1

The radius r of a cylinder is given as $2 \cdot 1 \pm 0 \cdot 1$ cm and the length l as $6 \cdot 4 \pm 0 \cdot 2$ cm. Find the volume of the cylinder and its standard error.

The volume V cm^3 of the cylinder is given by

$$V = \pi(2 \cdot 1)^2 6 \cdot 4 \pm \alpha$$

where $\qquad \left(\dfrac{\alpha}{V}\right)^2 = \left(\dfrac{2\alpha_1}{r}\right)^2 + \left(\dfrac{\alpha_2}{l}\right)^2,$

and α_1 and α_2 are the standard errors of r and l respectively

therefore $\qquad \left(\dfrac{\alpha}{V}\right)^2 = \left(\dfrac{0 \cdot 2}{2 \cdot 1}\right)^2 + \left(\dfrac{0 \cdot 2}{6 \cdot 4}\right)^2$

$$= \frac{4}{441} + \frac{1}{1024}$$

$$= 0 \cdot 0090 + 0 \cdot 0010 = 0 \cdot 0101$$

that is $\qquad \alpha/V = 0 \cdot 10$

Hence $\qquad V = \pi(2 \cdot 1)^2 6 \cdot 4(1 \pm 0 \cdot 10)$

$$= 88 \cdot 7 \pm 8 \cdot 9$$

EXAMPLE 2

The refractive index n of the glass of a prism is given by $n = \sin \frac{1}{2}(A + D)/\sin \frac{1}{2}A$ where A is the angle of the prism and D is the angle of minimum deviation. The results of several measurements of A and D are given as $A = 60° \ 5 \cdot 2' \pm 0 \cdot 2'$ and $D = 46° \ 36 \cdot 6' \pm 0 \cdot 4'$. Find the refractive index of the prism for the particular wavelength of light used.

Taking $\frac{1}{2}(A + D) = 53° \ 20 \cdot 9'$ and $\frac{1}{2}A = 30° \ 2 \cdot 6'$ we have $n = 0 \cdot 802\,280/0 \cdot 500\,655 = 1 \cdot 602\,46.$

To find the standard error we have

$$\frac{\partial n}{\partial A} = \frac{\frac{1}{2}\sin \frac{1}{2}A \cos \frac{1}{2}(A + D) - \frac{1}{2}\sin \frac{1}{2}(A + D)\cos \frac{1}{2}A}{\sin^2 \frac{1}{2}A}$$

$$= -\frac{\sin \frac{1}{2}D}{2\sin^2 \frac{1}{2}A} = -\frac{\sin \frac{1}{2}D}{1 - \cos A} = -\frac{\sin 23° \ 18 \cdot 3'}{1 - \cos 60° \ 5 \cdot 2'} = -0 \cdot 79$$

Also
$$\frac{\partial n}{\partial D} = \frac{\frac{1}{2}\cos\frac{1}{2}(A + D)}{\sin\frac{1}{2}A} = \frac{\cos 53° 20·9'}{2\sin 30° 2·6'}$$
$$= \frac{0·597}{1·00} = 0·60$$

But $\alpha_A = \pm 0·2' = \pm 0·000058$ radian

and $\alpha_B = \pm 0·4' = \pm 0·000116$ radian

Hence the standard error α of n is given by
$$\alpha^2 = (0·79 \times 0·58 \times 10^{-4})^2 + (0·60 \times 1·16 \times 10^{-4})^2$$
$$= 0·69 \times 10^{-8}$$
therefore $\alpha = \pm 0·83 \times 10^{-4}$

Hence the refractive index of the glass of the prism
$$= 1·60246 \pm 0·00008$$

EXERCISES 4

1. Certain observations of the right ascension of Polaris have been grouped[16] as follows, where x denotes the deviation in seconds of time from a value near the mean of the observations and y denotes the number of observations having a deviation x. Fit a normal error curve to these observations. Plot the curve and draw the histogram of the observations on the same figure.

x	$-3·5$	$-3·0$	$-2·5$	$-2·0$	$-1·5$	$-1·0$	$-0·5$
y	2	12	25	43	74	126	150

x	0	0·5	1·0	1·5	2·5	3·0	3·5
y	168	148	129	78	33	10	2

2. Twenty measurements of the acceleration due to gravity were found to have a mean value of $9·811 \text{ m s}^{-2}$ with a standard deviation of $0·014$. Another thirty had a mean value of $9·802 \text{ m s}^{-2}$ with a standard deviation of $0·022$. Assuming the two sets of measurements belong to the same normal population, find the mean of the fifty measurements and its standard error. What are the limits of uncertainty in this standard error?

3. Fifteen measurements of the surface tension of water have a mean value of $0.072\,52$ N m^{-1} with a standard deviation of $0.000\,64$. Find the standard error of the mean and its uncertainty. Given that the accepted value of the surface tension at the temperature of the laboratory is $0.073\,05$ N m^{-1} show that there is likely to be a systematic error in the measurements.

4. The results of determinations of a physical quantity by two different methods were quoted as $15 + x$ units, where $100\,x$ had the following values:

    (a) 37, 39, 38, 37, 39, 40, 41, 37, 36, 39

    (b) 40, 39, 41, 42, 40, 43, 38, 41, 40, 38.

Is there evidence that the two sets of values differ systematically from one another?

5. If $m = 0.850 \pm 0.012$ find m^2, m^3 and $1/m$.

6. If $a = 1.16 \pm 0.08$ and $b = 2.54 \pm 0.12$ find $a + b$, ab, a/b, $(b - a)/a$ and $\log_e a$.

7. If $\quad v = 0.4107 \pm 0.0003$ m, $\quad u = 0.3513 \pm 0.0002$ m $\quad$ and $1/f = 1/v + 1/u$, calculate f and its standard error.

8. The refractive index n of the glass of a double convex lens is calculated from the formula $1/f = (n - 1)(1/r_1 - 1/r_2)$. If $\quad r_1 = 0.312 \pm 0.001$ m, $\quad r_2 = 1.490 \pm 0.005$ m $\quad$ and $f = 0.501 \pm 0.002$ m, find n.

9. Given that
$$e/m = (1.7592 \pm 0.0005) \times 10^{11} \text{ C kg}^{-1}$$
$$e = (1.602\,03 \pm 0.000\,34) \times 10^{-19} \text{ C}$$
calculate the electronic mass m.

10. Given that

$$c = (2.997\,76 \pm 0.000\,04) \times 10^8 \text{ m s}^{-1}$$
$$R_\infty = 109\,737\,30 \pm 5 \text{ m}^{-1}$$
$$m = (9.1091 \pm 0.0005) \times 10^{-31} \text{ kg}$$
$$e = (1.602\,10 \pm 0.000\,52) \times 10^{-19} \text{ C}$$
$$\epsilon_0 = (8.854\,18 \pm 0.000\,04) \times 10^{-12} \text{ kg}^{-1} \text{ m}^{-3} \text{ s}^2\text{c}^2$$

find Planck's constant h, using the relation
$$h^3 = me^4/8\epsilon_0^2 R_\infty c.$$

40. Method of least squares

The **principle of least squares,** which was first formulated by Legendre, may be expressed as follows:

the most probable value of any observed quantity is such that the sum of the squares of the deviations of the observations from this value is least.

If $x_1, x_2, ---, x_n$ are observed values of any given quantity, then according to the principle of least squares the most probable value of this quantity is X chosen so that

$$(x_1 - X)^2 + (x_2 - X)^2 + \cdots + (x_n - X)^2$$

is least.

Now if $\bar{x}$ is the mean of $x_1, x_2, ---, x_n$ so that $\Sigma x_s = n\bar{x}$ or $\Sigma(x_s - \bar{x}) = 0$ we have

$$\Sigma(x_s - X)^2 = \Sigma[(x_s - \bar{x}) + (\bar{x} - X)]^2$$
$$= \Sigma(x_s - \bar{x})^2 + n(\bar{x} - X)^2$$

which is clearly least when $X = \bar{x}$.

Thus applying the principle of least squares we derive the result that **the most probable value of a measured quantity is the arithmetic mean of the observations.**

More generally, if the observations $x_1, x_2, ---, x_n$ occur with frequencies $f_1, f_2, ---, f_n$ respectively, then applying the principle of least squares the most probable value of the measured quantity is X, such that

$$f_1(x_1 - X)^2 + f_2(x_2 - X)^2 + \cdots + f_n(x_n - X)^2$$

is least.

If now we write $\bar{x} = \Sigma f_s x_s / \Sigma f_s$, that is, the mean of the observations each "weighted" according to the frequency of its occurrence, we have

$$\Sigma f_s(x_s - \bar{x}) = 0$$
and hence $\quad \Sigma f_s(x_s - X)^2 = \Sigma f_s[(x_s - \bar{x}) + (\bar{x} - X)]^2$
$$= \Sigma f_s(x_s - \bar{x})^2 + (\bar{x} - X)^2 \Sigma f$$

This is clearly least when $X = \bar{x}$.

Thus the most probable value of the measured quantity is the **weighted** mean of the observations, that is,

$$(f_1 x_1 + f_2 x_2 + \cdots + f_n x_n)/(f_1 + f_2 + \cdots + f_n)$$

In such an expression f_s is known as the **weight** of the observation x .

If **all** the weights are multiplied by the same constant factor the value of the weighted mean is unchanged. In the above derivation the weight equals the frequency of occurrence of the observation, but other significances are given to the weight often depending upon the personal assessment of the observer. Sometimes the weight attributed to any observation is determined, as explained later, by the accuracy of the observation.

41. Weighted mean

Both Laplace and Gauss using different techniques established the principle of least squares mathematically. We have mentioned earlier that Gauss, assuming that the mean of the observations is the most probable value of a measured quantity, deduced the normal error law. Conversely, we can use the normal error law to deduce that the most probable value is the mean. The "proof" proceeds as follows:

The probability of the occurrence of an observation x_1 is given by

$$(h/\sqrt{\pi})\, e^{-h^2(x_1 - x)^2}$$

where x is the magnitude of the measured quantity.

Hence the probability of the occurrence of the observations $x_1, x_2, \text{- - -}, x_n$, being the product of the probabilities of the occurrence of each separately, equals

$$(h/\sqrt{\pi})^n\, e^{-h^2 \Sigma (x_s - x)^2}$$

if we assume that all the observations belong to the same Gaussian population specified by the precision constant h.

Thus the probability is a maximum if $\Sigma(x_s - x)^2$ is a minimum, in keeping with the principle of least squares. As we have shown above this occurs when x is the mean of $x_1, x_2, \text{- - -}, x_n$.

It may be, of course, that the measurements $x_1, x_2, \text{- - -}, x_n$ belong to different Gaussian populations; the accuracy of measurement may be different in each case.

We can then write the probability of the observation x_s as

$$(h_s/\sqrt{\pi})\, e^{-h_s^2(x_s - x)^2}$$

and hence the probability of the occurrence of the observations $x_1, x_2, \text{- - -}, x_n$ as

$$h_1 h_2 \text{- - -} h_n \pi^{-\frac{1}{2}n}\, e^{-\Sigma h_s^2 (x_s - x)^2}$$

This is greatest when $\Sigma h_s^2(x_s - x)^2$ is least, which occurs when x is given by the weighted mean $\Sigma h_s^2 x_s / \Sigma h_s^2$. The proof is exactly as given above.

If we write $h_s^2 = 1/2\sigma_s^2$ as quoted in Section 25, the most probable value of a measured quantity deducible from the observations $x_1, x_2, \text{- - -}, x_n$ is given by

$$\frac{\Sigma h_s^2 x_s}{\Sigma h_s^2} = \frac{\Sigma x_s / \sigma_s^2}{\Sigma 1 / \sigma_s^2}$$

This reduces, of course, to the arithmetic mean if $\sigma_1 = \sigma_2 = \text{- - -} = \sigma_n$.

Combining this result with that obtained above, it is clear that if the observations $x_1 x_2, \text{- - -}, x_n$ occur with frequencies $f_1, f_2, \text{- - -}, f_n$ or if x_s is the mean of f_s observations, then the most probable value of the measured quantity is

$$\frac{\Sigma h_s^2 f_s x_s}{\Sigma h_s^2 f_s} = \frac{\Sigma f_s x_s / \sigma_s^2}{\Sigma f_s / \sigma_s^2} = \frac{\Sigma x_s / \alpha_s^2}{\Sigma 1 / \alpha_s^2}$$

where $\alpha_s = \sigma_s / \sqrt{f_s}$ and represents the standard error of the mean (cf. Section 29) corresponding to the observations x_s. **Thus each observation x_s can be given a weight proportional to the reciprocal of the square of its standard error.** Alternatively, since the probable error is a constant multiple of the standard error a weight proportional to the reciprocal of the square of the probable error may be used.

42. Standard error of weighted mean

Quite generally, if the observations $x_1, x_2, \text{- - -}, x_n$ are given the weights $w_1, w_2, \text{- - -}, w_n$ respectively the weighted mean is $\bar{x} = \Sigma w_s x_s / \Sigma w_s$. As proved earlier, the sum $\Sigma w_s(x_s - X)^2$ is least when X equals this weighted mean, $\bar{x}$.

To estimate the accuracy of the weighted mean we find the quantity σ^2 given by

$$\sigma^2 = \sum_{s-1}^{n} w_s(x_s - \bar{x})^2 / (n - 1)$$

This is the variance with which the quantities $w_s^{\frac{1}{2}}(x_s - \bar{x})$ are distributed about zero. It can be shown that the standard error of the weighted mean is given by $\sigma/(\Sigma w_s)^{\frac{1}{2}}$, that is,

$$\left[\frac{\Sigma w_s(x_s - \bar{x})^2}{(n-1)\Sigma w_s}\right]^{\frac{1}{2}}$$

If all the weights are equal this reduces to

$$\left[\frac{\Sigma(x_s - \bar{x})^2}{(n-1)n}\right]^{\frac{1}{2}}$$

in keeping with the usual formula.   (Section 30.)

EXAMPLE 1

Find the most probable value of a quantity of which the following are observed values: $9\cdot4, 9\cdot3, 9\cdot4, 9\cdot5, 9\cdot6, 9\cdot3, 9\cdot7, 9\cdot5, 9\cdot2, 9\cdot4$.

Treating the observations as of equal weight, the most probable value is given by the arithmetic mean, which equals $9 + \frac{1}{10}(4\cdot3) = 9\cdot43$.

To find the standard error of the mean we calculate σ^2; using $9\cdot4$ as the mean we get

$$\sigma^2 = 0\cdot28/9 = 0\cdot031$$

If we used $9\cdot43$ as the mean we would get

$$\sigma^2 = 0\cdot031 - (0\cdot03)^2 = 0\cdot030$$

The standard error of the mean $= \sqrt{0\cdot030}/\sqrt{10} = 0\cdot055$.

The mean is therefore $9\cdot43 \pm 0\cdot06$, but in view of the accuracy of the given values one might be inclined to write the mean as $9\cdot4 \pm 0\cdot1$. This would be misleading, however, especially if the number of observations were not quoted. It has to be remembered that the accuracy of the standard error is not very high when the number of observations is small. For as we have stated earlier (Section 30) the standard error of the standard deviation is $\sigma/\sqrt{[2(n-1)]}$, so that the standard error of the mean, $\sigma/\sqrt{n}$, is sometimes written as

$$\frac{\sigma}{\sqrt{n}}\left\{1 \pm \frac{1}{\sqrt{[2(n-1)]}}\right\}$$

which in this case equals $0\cdot055(1 \pm 0\cdot24)$.

It is therefore usually recommended that in computations of this kind two doubtful figures should be retained and the standard (or probable) error expressed to two significant figures. Accordingly the above result should be written $9 \cdot 430 \pm 0 \cdot 055$ (10 observations) or $9 \cdot 430 \pm 0 \cdot 055(1 \pm 0 \cdot 24)$. Jeffreys has written "if anybody wants to reduce a good set of observations to meaninglessness he can hardly do better than to round the uncertainty to one figure and suppress the number of observations."

EXAMPLE 2

The observations x_s and their weights w_s are given below. Find the most probable value of the measured quantity and the standard error.

x_s	w_s	$w_s(x_s - 10)$	d_s	d_s^2	$w_s d_s^2$
10·25	1	0·25	−0·06	0·0036	0·0036
10·32	2	0·64	0·01	0·0001	0·0002
10·43	4	1·72	0·12	0·0144	0·0576
10·27	3	0·81	−0·04	0·0016	0·0048
10·16	2	0·32	−0·15	0·0225	0·0450
sum	12	3·74			0·1112

The most probable value is the weighted mean given by $\bar{x} = \Sigma w_s x_s / \Sigma w_s$, that is, $10 + 3 \cdot 74/12 = 10 \cdot 312$.

Also the standard error of the mean is given by $\sigma/(\Sigma w_s)^{\frac{1}{2}}$, where

$$\sigma^2 = \sum_{s=1}^{n} w_s d_s^2/(n-1)$$

$$d_s = x_s - \bar{x}$$

and n is the number of observations.

Hence from the above table taking $\bar{x} = 10 \cdot 31$ we have

$$\sigma^2 = 0 \cdot 1112/4 = 0 \cdot 0278$$

therefore $\sigma = 0 \cdot 167$

and the standard error of the mean $= 0 \cdot 167/\sqrt{12} = 0 \cdot 048$.

We can write the measured quantity as $10 \cdot 31 \pm 0 \cdot 05$ or preferably $10 \cdot 312 \pm 0 \cdot 048$ (5 observations).

EXAMPLE 3

Values of the ratio e/m for the electron as determined by different methods are given below along with the probable error of each value. Find the most probable value of e/m and the standard error.

$(e/m) \times 10^{-11}$	Probable error
1·761 10	10·0 × 10⁻⁴
1·759 00	9·0 × 10⁻⁴
1·759 82	4·0 × 10⁻⁴
1·758 20	13·0 × 10⁻⁴
1·758 70	8·0 × 10⁻⁴

We will take the weight of each determination as inversely proportional to the square of the probable error; these values w_s are given in column 1 below. In column 2 are the values of $x_s = (e/m) \times 10^{-11} - 1·75800$ corresponding to a working mean of $1·758\,00$. The necessary working is given below.

w_s	$x_s \times 10^5$	$w_s x_s \times 10^5$	$d_s \times 10^5$	$d_s^2 \times 10^8$	$w_s d_s^2 \times 10^8$
1·0	310	310	151	228	228
1·2	100	120	− 59	35	42
6·3	182	1147	23	5	32
0·6	20	12	−139	193	116
1·6	70	112	− 89	79	126
10·7		1701			544

Hence omitting the factor 10^{-11} we have:

$$\text{weighted mean} = 1·758\,00 + \frac{0·017\,01}{10·7} = 1·759\,59$$

Therefore, writing $d_s = (e/m) \times 10^{-11} - 1·759\,59$ we get as shown above

$$\sigma^2 = 0·000\,005\,44/4 = 0·000\,001\,36$$

Standard error of the mean $= \sqrt{(0·000\,001\,36/10·7)} = 0·000\,36$. Hence $e/m = (1·759\,59 \pm 0·000\,36) \times 10^{11}$ C kg⁻¹.

43. Internal and external consistency

If the weight w_s assigned to the observation x_s is proportional to $1/\alpha_s^2$, where α_s is the standard error of x_s, the standard error α of the weighted mean $\bar{x}$ may be found as explained in Section 42, and is given by

$$\alpha^2 = \frac{\Sigma(x_s - \bar{x})^2/\alpha_s^2}{(n-1)\Sigma 1/\alpha_s^2} \tag{12}$$

But it is possible to derive another expression for the standard error as follows. We have

$$\bar{x} = \Sigma k_s x_s \quad \text{where} \quad k_s = w_s/\Sigma w_s$$

and hence using equation (11) of Section 37, the standard error of $\bar{x}$ is α where

$$\alpha^2 = \Sigma k_s^2 \alpha_s^2 = \Sigma w_s^2 \alpha_s^2/(\Sigma w_s)^2$$

If w_s is proportional to $1/\alpha_s^2$ this reduces to

$$\alpha^2 = (\Sigma 1/\alpha_s^2)/(\Sigma 1/\alpha_s^2)^2 = 1/(\Sigma 1/\alpha_s^2) \tag{13}$$

Now expressions (12) and (13) are apparently quite different. We note that expression (13) depends entirely on the standard errors of the separate observations, whereas expression (12) depends also upon the differences between the observations. The latter is therefore a function of what might be called, following Birge, the "external" consistency of the observations, whereas expression (13) depends upon the "internal" consistency. We shall denote the standard errors obtained using expressions (12) and (13) by α_e and α_i respectively. For samples taken from an infinite normal population it may be shown that α_e and α_i are equal, or more strictly, the ratio α_e/α_i is unity with standard error $1/\sqrt{[2(n-1)]}$. We note that

$$Z = \frac{\alpha_e}{\alpha_i} = \left[\frac{\sum_{s=1}^{n} (x_s - \bar{x})^2/\alpha_s^2}{(n-1)} \right]^{\frac{1}{2}}$$

In practice it will be found that Z does not equal unity. This is not surprising, for it depends on the values of α_s, some or all of which may be considerably inaccurate especially if they have been calculated from few observations. Further, Z depends as well on the values of $(x_s - \bar{x})^2$ and so will be affected by any systematic errors present.

If, however, this ratio is found not to differ from unity significantly, having in mind the uncertainties in the standard errors used, then the observations as a whole may be regarded as consistent. In such a case it is perhaps safer to choose the larger of the values of α_e and α_i as the standard error of the weighted mean.

If, on the other hand, α_e/α_i differs from unity by an amount much greater than is to be expected on the basis of statistical fluctuations, it may be concluded that systematic errors are likely to be present. In such a situation the weights based on the standard errors should be discarded and replaced by others. The assignment of new weights must be somewhat arbitrary, depending inevitably upon the judgment of the individual concerned and his knowledge of the experimental conditions.

In Example 3 above we have shown that equation (12) leads to the result $\alpha_e = 0 \cdot 000\,36$. If we use equation (13) we have

$$\Sigma 1/\alpha_s^2 = r^2 \times 10^8(0 \cdot 010 + 0 \cdot 012 + 0 \cdot 063 + 0 \cdot 006 + 0 \cdot 016)$$
$$= r^2 \times 10^8 \times 0 \cdot 107$$

where $r = 0 \cdot 6745$, the ratio of the probable error to the standard error.

Hence $\qquad \alpha_i = r^{-1} \times 10^{-4}/\sqrt{0 \cdot 107} = 0 \cdot 000\,45$

Consequently $Z = 36/45 = 0 \cdot 8$, from which we may conclude that the values are consistent, for with $n = 10$ the uncertainty in Z is about $0 \cdot 24$. We might therefore safely take α equal to $0 \cdot 000\,45$, that is, $e/m = (1 \cdot 759\,59 \pm 0 \cdot 000\,45)10^7$ e.m.u.g^{-1}.

EXERCISES 5

1. Show that the mean of p equally good observations has a weight p times that of one of them.

2. Find the area under the curve $y = x^2$ from $x = 0$ to $x = 8$ by calculating y when $x = 0, 2, 4, 6, 8$ and giving these ordinates (i) equal weights, (ii) weights 1, 2, 2, 2, 1 respectively, and (iii) weights 1, 4, 2, 4, 1 respectively.

3. The refractive index of a glass prism was found successively to be $1 \cdot 53$, $1 \cdot 57$, $1 \cdot 54$, $1 \cdot 54$, $1 \cdot 50$, $1 \cdot 51$, $1 \cdot 55$, $1 \cdot 54$, $1 \cdot 56$ and $1 \cdot 53$. Find the mean and its standard error if the observations are given (a) equal weights, (b) weights 1, 2, 3, 3, 1, 1, 3, 3, 2, 1 respectively.

4. Ten observations of a quantity have a mean of $9 \cdot 52$ and standard error $0 \cdot 08$; another 20 observations of the same quantity have a mean of $9 \cdot 49$ and standard error $0 \cdot 05$. Find the mean and standard error of the 30 observations using weights (i) proportional to the number of observations, and (ii) inversely proportional to the square of the standard errors.

5. Two groups of determinations of e/m for the electron give the following values: $1 \cdot 758\,80 \pm 0 \cdot 000\,42$ and $1 \cdot 759\,59 \pm 0 \cdot 000\,36$, the unit being 10^{11} C kg^{-1}. Find the weighted mean of these values and its standard error.

6. Two determinations of the Faraday constant are: $96\,497 \cdot 6 \pm 6 \cdot 3$ and $96\,506 \cdot 6 \pm 7 \cdot 7$ C mol^{-1}. Find the difference of these two values and its standard error.

   Find also the weighted mean of the two values and its standard error. Test for internal and external consistency.

7. Test the following results for external and internal consistency:
   (a) 10 ± 1, 11 ± 2, 12 ± 1 and 15 ± 2.
   (b) $10 \cdot 1 \pm 1 \cdot 2$, $11 \cdot 4 \pm 2 \cdot 4$, $12 \cdot 2 \pm 1 \cdot 3$ and $14 \cdot 9 \pm 1 \cdot 7$.

8. Four determinations of Planck's constant h were rounded off and given with their probable errors as

$$6 \cdot 557 \pm 0 \cdot 006$$
$$6 \cdot 554 \pm 0 \cdot 007$$
$$6 \cdot 546 \pm 0 \cdot 010$$
and
$$6 \cdot 544 \pm 0 \cdot 009$$

   the unit being 10^{-34} Js. Find the most probable value of h and its standard error.

   Repeat the calculations using the original values

$$6 \cdot 5568 \pm 0 \cdot 0063$$
$$6 \cdot 5539 \pm 0 \cdot 0072$$
$$6 \cdot 5464 \pm 0 \cdot 0095$$
and
$$6 \cdot 5443 \pm 0 \cdot 0091$$

9. A precision method of finding the diffusivity p of nickel resulted in the following values with their probable errors:

$$0 \cdot 004\,218\,4 \pm 0 \cdot 000\,0021 \text{ s}^{-1}$$
$$4\,206\,8 \pm \qquad 78$$
$$4\,221\,3 \pm \qquad 18$$
$$4\,209\,3 \pm \qquad 35$$
$$4\,228\,1 \pm \qquad 57$$
$$4\,214\,8 \pm \qquad 71$$
$$4\,213\,5 \pm \qquad 30$$

Find the most probable value of p and its standard error.

10. Values of the velocity of light in kilometres per second as corrected by Birge[12] are given below:

Author	Epoch	Corrected result	Probable error
Rosa-Dorsey	1906·0	299 784	10
Mercier	1923·0	299 782	30
Michelson	1926·5	299 798	15
Mittelstadt	1928·0	299 786	10
Michelson, Pease and Pearson	1932·5	299 774	4
Anderson	1936·8	299 771	10
Huttel	1937·0	299 771	10
Anderson	1940·0	299 776	6

Find the weighted mean and its standard error. Test for internal and external consistency.

11. Twelve precision values of e/m for the electron obtained by seven essentially different methods are given below, the unit being 10^{11} C kg^{-1}. Find the weighted mean and standard error of (i) all twelve values, and (ii) of the first six (the "spectroscopic" values). Test for internal and external consistency in each case.

	e/m	Probable error $\times 10^4$
1	1·75913	3·7
2	1·74797	5·0
3	1·75914	5·0
4	1·75815	6·0
5	1·76048	5·8
6	1·75700	7·0
7	1·76006	4·0
8	1·76110	10·0
9	1·75900	9·0
10	1·75982	4·0
11	1·75820	13·0
12	1·75870	8·0

12. Given that the probability of the occurrence of the set of measurements $x_1, x_2, - - -, x_n$ is proportional to

$$P = (h/\sqrt{\pi})^n \, e^{-h^2\Sigma(x_s - \bar{x})^2}$$

where $\bar{x}$ is the arithmetic mean of the measurements, find the value of h for which P is a maximum.

44. Other applications of the method of least squares; solution of linear equations

Legendre applied the method of least squares to the following problem.

Suppose we have a number of linear equations in the two variables x and y of the form

$$a_s x + b_s y = k_s$$

where a_s, b_s, k_s are constants. Suppose there are n equations where $n > 2$.

Values of x and y can be found that satisfy *any* two of the equations. These values may not satisfy *all* the equations, that is, the equations may not be consistent. In this case the question arises: what are the values of x and y that satisfy all the equations as closely as possible?

The method of least squares can be applied to the solution of this problem. For writing

$$a_s x + b_s y - k_s = e_s$$

we can choose x and y such that the sum of the squares of the "errors" e_s is least.

Thus $$\sum_{s=1}^{n} (a_s x + b_s y - k_s)^2$$

must be a minimum.

Differentiating partially with respect to x and y we get as necessary conditions for a minimum:

$$\Sigma a_s(a_s x + b_s y - k_s) = 0$$
and $$\Sigma b_s(a_s x + b_s y - k_s) = 0$$

From these two equations the values of x and y can be found. These are the "most probable" values.

The above equations are usually written in the form

$$[aa]x + [ab]y - [ak] = 0 \tag{14}$$
$$[ab]x + [bb]y - [bk] = 0 \tag{15}$$

where $[ab]$ denotes the summation $\sum_{s=1}^{n} a_s b_s$.

They are known as the **normal equations.**

96

In determinantal notation we can write

$$\frac{x}{\begin{vmatrix} [ak] & [ab] \\ [bk] & [bb] \end{vmatrix}} = \frac{y}{\begin{vmatrix} [aa] & [ak] \\ [ab] & [bk] \end{vmatrix}} = \frac{1}{\begin{vmatrix} [aa] & [ab] \\ [ab] & [bb] \end{vmatrix}}$$

If different weights can be assigned to the given equations and w_s is the weight of the equation $a_s x + b_s y = k_s$, then the normal equations become

$$[waa]x + [wab]y - [wak] = 0$$
$$[wab]x + [wbb]y - [wbk] = 0$$

It is clear from these equations that if each of the original equations is multiplied throughout by the **square root** of its weight the equations can be regarded as of equal weight.

EXAMPLE 1

Find the most probable values of x and y from the equations $2x + y = 5\cdot1$, $x - y = 1\cdot1$, $4x - y = 7\cdot2$ and $x + 4y = 5\cdot9$

We first construct the following table from the coefficients a_s, b_s, k_s of the given equations.

	a_s	b_s	k_s	a_s^2	$a_s b_s$	b_s^2	$a_s k_s$	$b_s k_s$
	2	1	5·1	4	2	1	10·2	5·1
	1	−1	1·1	1	−1	1	1·1	− 1·1
	4	−1	7·2	16	−4	1	28·8	− 7·2
	1	4	5·9	1	4	16	5·9	23·6
sum	8	3	19·3	22	1	19	46·0	20·4

Thus the normal equations are

$$22x + y = 46\cdot0$$
$$x + 19y = 20\cdot4$$

Solving we get $\quad x = \dfrac{874\cdot0 - 20\cdot4}{418 - 1} = \dfrac{853\cdot6}{417} = 2\cdot047$

and $\quad y = \dfrac{448\cdot8 - 46\cdot0}{418 - 1} = \dfrac{402\cdot8}{417} = 0\cdot966$

The most probable values are $x = 2\cdot05$ and $y = 0\cdot97$. With more complicated examples certain arithmetical checks are introduced.

EXAMPLE 2

Find the most probable values of x and y from the equations

$$2x + y = 5 \cdot 1, \; x - y = 1 \cdot 1 \text{ and } 4x - y = 7 \cdot 2$$

given that these equations have weights 1, 3 and 2 respectively.

We construct the following table:

w_s	a_s	b_s	k_s	wa_s^2	wa_sb_s	wb^2	wa_sk_s	wb_sk_s
1	2	1	$5 \cdot 1$	4	2	1	$10 \cdot 2$	$5 \cdot 1$
3	1	-1	$1 \cdot 1$	3	-3	3	$3 \cdot 3$	$-3 \cdot 3$
2	4	-1	$7 \cdot 2$	32	-8	2	$57 \cdot 6$	$-14 \cdot 4$
sum				39	-9	6	$71 \cdot 1$	$-12 \cdot 6$

Thus the normal equations are

$$39x - 9y = 71 \cdot 1$$

$$-9x + 6y = -12 \cdot 6$$

Solving we get $x = 2 \cdot 05$ and $y = 0 \cdot 97$

The most probable values are therefore $x = 2 \cdot 05$ and $y = 0 \cdot 97$.

EXAMPLE 3

The lengths AB, BC, CD, DE along a straight line are measured as $24 \cdot 1$, $35 \cdot 8$, $30 \cdot 3$ and $33 \cdot 8$ cm, but it is known that AD is accurately 90 cm and BE is 100 cm. Find the most probable values of AB, BC, CD, DE.

Let the lengths of AB, BC, CD, DE be x_1, x_2, x_3, x_4 cm respectively. Then writing

$$x_1 = 24 \cdot 1 + e_1, \; x_2 = 35 \cdot 8 + e_2, \; x_3 = 30 \cdot 3 + e_3, \; x_4 = 33 \cdot 8 + e_4$$

we have $e_1 + e_2 + e_3 = -0 \cdot 2$ (16)

$$e_2 + e_3 + e_4 = 0 \cdot 1 \tag{17}$$

We choose e_1, e_2, e_3, e_4 so that $e_1^2 + e_2^2 + e_3^2 + e_4^2$ is a minimum, whence

$$e_1de_1 + e_2de_2 + e_3de_3 + e_4de_4 = 0 \tag{18}$$

But from equations (1) and (2) we have

$$de_1 + de_2 + de_3 = 0 \qquad (19)$$

$$de_2 + de_3 + de_4 = 0 \qquad (20)$$

On multiplying* equations (19) and (20) by the undetermined multipliers λ_1 and λ_2 and adding we get

$$\lambda_1 de_1 + (\lambda_1 + \lambda_2)de_2 + (\lambda_1 + \lambda_2)de_3 + \lambda_2 de_4 = 0$$

Comparing this with equation (18) we have

$$\frac{e_1}{\lambda_1} = \frac{e_2}{\lambda_1 + \lambda_2} = \frac{e_3}{\lambda_1 + \lambda_2} = \frac{e_4}{\lambda_2}$$

so that $e_3 = e_2$ and $e_4 = e_2 - e_1$

Hence on substituting in equations (16) and (17) we get

$$e_1 + 2e_2 = -0 \cdot 2$$

$$-e_1 + 3e_2 = 0 \cdot 1$$

Hence $e_1 = -0 \cdot 16$ and $e_2 = -0 \cdot 02$

therefore $e_3 = -0 \cdot 02$ and $e_4 = 0 \cdot 14$

Hence the most probable values are

$$x_1 = 23 \cdot 9, \quad x_2 = 35 \cdot 8, \quad x_3 = 30 \cdot 3, \quad x_4 = 33 \cdot 9$$

45. Solution of linear equations involving observed quantities

In Section 44 we considered the problem of finding the most probable values of x and y from $n(> 2)$ linear equations $a_s x + b_s y = k_s$.

Now let us suppose that the constants a_s, b_s are known accurately but the constants k_s are subject to accidental errors of observation. Also let us suppose the equations have been multiplied by the square roots of their weights, so that the weight of each may be taken as unity.

* In mathematics this method of solution is often referred to as the method of undetermined multipliers.

Then, as before, the most probable values of x and y are the solutions of the normal equations

$$[aa]x + [ab]y = [ak]$$
$$[ab]x + [bb]y = [bk]$$

Gauss[17] and others have discussed the problem of estimating the weights that may be assigned to the values of x and y so obtained. Denoting these values by x_0 and y_0 and writing $a_s x_0 + b_s y_0 - k_s = d_s$, that is, $d_1 d_2, - - -, d_n$ are the residuals when the most probable values x_0 and y_0 are substituted in the given equations, it has been shown that the standard error α to be expected in any expression $a_s x_0 + b_s y_0 - k_s$ is given by*

$$\alpha^2 = [dd]/(n - 2)$$

Also if α_x and α_y denote the standard errors in x_0 and y_0 respectively, then it can be shown that

$$\frac{\alpha_x^2}{[bb]} = \frac{\alpha_y^2}{[aa]} = \frac{\alpha^2}{\Delta}$$

where Δ is the determinant

$$\begin{vmatrix} [aa] & [ab] \\ [ab] & [bb] \end{vmatrix}$$

If, as an example, we consider the equations solved in Example 1, Section 44, namely,

$$2x + y = 5 \cdot 1, \quad x - y = 1 \cdot 1, \quad 4x - y = 7 \cdot 2 \text{ and } x + 4y = 5 \cdot 9$$

the normal equations are

$$22x + y = 46 \cdot 0$$
$$x + 19y = 20 \cdot 4$$

leading to $x = 2 \cdot 05$ and $y = 0 \cdot 97$.

The residuals are therefore $-0 \cdot 03$, $-0 \cdot 02$, $0 \cdot 03$ and $0 \cdot 03$ so that $[dd] = 0 \cdot 0031$ and $\alpha^2 = 0 \cdot 001\,55$.

Hence
$$\frac{\alpha_x^2}{19} = \frac{\alpha_y^2}{22} = \frac{0 \cdot 001\,55}{417}$$

therefore $\quad\quad \alpha_x = 0 \cdot 008 \quad \text{and} \quad \alpha_y = 0 \cdot 009$

* If there are m unknowns $x, y, - - -$ the denominator is $(n - m)$.

We can write $x = 2 \cdot 05 \pm 0 \cdot 01$ and $y = 0 \cdot 97 \pm 0 \cdot 01$.

As a further example, let us suppose that by direct observation it has been found independently that

$$x = 1 \cdot 00 \pm 0 \cdot 10 \quad \text{and} \quad y = 0 \cdot 90 \pm 0 \cdot 07$$

Further, suppose that a third independent observation leads to

$$x + 2y = 3 \cdot 00 \pm 0 \cdot 07$$

What are the most probable values of x and y?

We will give the equations weights inversely proportional to the squares of their standard errors, namely, 1, 2, 2. So multiplying the equations by 1, $\sqrt{2}$, $\sqrt{2}$ respectively we get

$$x = 1 \cdot 00, \quad y\sqrt{2} = 0 \cdot 90\sqrt{2} \quad \text{and} \quad x\sqrt{2} + 2y\sqrt{2} = 3 \cdot 00\sqrt{2}$$

each of which can now be regarded as having unit weight. We therefore have

a_s	b_s	k_s	a^2	b_s^2	$a_s b_s$	$a_s k_s$	$b_s k_s$
1	0	$1 \cdot 00$	1	0	0	$1 \cdot 00$	0
0	$\sqrt{2}$	$0 \cdot 90\sqrt{2}$	0	2	0	0	$1 \cdot 80$
$\sqrt{2}$	$2\sqrt{2}$	$3 \cdot 00\sqrt{2}$	2	8	4	$6 \cdot 00$	$12 \cdot 00$
sum			3	10	4	$7 \cdot 00$	$13 \cdot 80$

The normal equations are

$$3x + 4y = 7 \cdot 00$$
$$4x + 10y = 13 \cdot 80$$

leading to $x = 1 \cdot 057$ and $y = 0 \cdot 957$.

Using $x = 1 \cdot 06$ and $y = 0 \cdot 96$ we get

$$[dd] = 0 \cdot 0036 + 0 \cdot 0072 + 0 \cdot 0008 = 0 \cdot 011$$

Hence $\qquad \alpha_x^2/10 = \alpha_y^2/3 = 0 \cdot 0116/14$

leading to $\qquad \alpha_x = 0 \cdot 09 \quad \text{and} \quad \alpha_y = 0 \cdot 05$

Hence $\qquad x = 1 \cdot 06 \pm 0 \cdot 09 \quad \text{and} \quad y = 0 \cdot 96 \pm 0 \cdot 05$

46. Curve fitting

Another useful application of the method of least squares is the fitting of a curve, or a theoretical formula, to a set of experimental data.

Suppose $y_1\, y_2, ---, y_n$ are the values of a measured quantity y (or combination of measured quantities) corresponding to the values $x_1, x_2, ---, x_n$ of another quantity x.

Let us assume, for simplicity, that there are experimental errors in the values of y_s but not in the values of x_s. Conditions closely approaching these, where the errors in one of the variables may be neglected, often occur in practice. We assume too there exists a linear relation between x and y, namely,

$$y = ax + b$$

On substituting $x = x_s$, the value of y will not in general equal y_s; there will be an "error" of amount

$$ax_s + b - y_s$$

To obtain the linear relation (or the line) which best fits the data we choose a and b such that the sum of the squares of the "errors" is least, that is,

$$\Sigma(ax_s + b - y_s)^2$$

is least.

The conditions obtained by differentiating partially with respect to a and b are

$$\Sigma x_s(ax_s + b - y_s) = 0$$

and

$$\Sigma(ax_s + b - y_s) = 0$$

Hence

$$a[xx] + b[x] = [xy] \tag{21}$$

$$a[x] + bn = [y] \tag{22}$$

which give

$$a = \frac{n[xy] - [x][y]}{n[xx] - [x][x]} \tag{23}$$

and

$$b = \frac{[y][xx] - [x][xy]}{n[xx] - [x][x]} \tag{24}$$

We note that if $b = 0$ we have $y = ax$

where

$$a = \frac{[xy]}{[xx]} = \frac{[y]}{[x]} \tag{25}$$

EXAMPLE

Fit a linear law to the values of x and y given in the following table, assuming the values of x are accurate.

x	y	xy	xx
0	4·6	0	0
1	7·1	7·1	1
2	9·5	19·0	4
3	11·5	34·5	9
4	13·7	54·8	16
5	15·9	79·5	25
6	18·6	111·6	36
7	20·9	146·3	49
8	23·5	188·0	64
9	25·4	228·6	81
sum 45	150·7	869·4	285

If the relation is $y = ax + b$ then from equations (23) and (24) we have

$$a = \frac{8694 - 45 \times 150 \cdot 7}{2850 - 45^2}$$

$$= \frac{1912 \cdot 5}{825} = 2 \cdot 32$$

and

$$b = \frac{150 \cdot 7 \times 285 - 45 \times 869 \cdot 4}{825}$$

$$= \frac{3826 \cdot 5}{825} = 4 \cdot 64$$

therefore

$$y = 2 \cdot 32x + 4 \cdot 64$$

It is instructive to plot the values of x and y, and to draw the straight line that fits the points best.

47. Line of regression

It is of interest to note that the second of the normal equations, equation (22) above, can be written as

$$a\frac{[x]}{n} + b = \frac{[y]}{n}$$

This indicates that the point $([x]/n, [y]/n)$ lies on the line $y = ax + b$, that is, the line passes through the point $(\bar{x}, \bar{y})$ where $\bar{x}$ and $\bar{y}$ are the arithmetic means of the values of x and y respectively.

In the example given above $\bar{x} = 4·5$ and $\bar{y} = 15·07$, and it can be verified that these co-ordinates satisfy very closely the equation $y = 2·32x + 4·64$.

It is therefore useful to write

$$x = \bar{x} + X \quad \text{and} \quad y = \bar{y} + Y$$

whence $Y = aX$ and hence from equation (25) above $a = [XY]/[XX]$.

The relation between x and y can therefore be written

$$y - \bar{y} = \frac{[XY]}{[XX]}(x - \bar{x})$$

If we write $[XX] = n\sigma_X^2$, $[YY] = n\sigma_Y^2$ and $r^2 = [XY]^2/[XX][YY]$

we have

$$\frac{y - \bar{y}}{\sigma_Y} = r\frac{x - \bar{x}}{\sigma_X}$$

This is known as the **line of regression** of y on x. We note that r has the same sign as $[XY]$ and hence the same sign as the gradient a.

Of course, it may happen that both sets of quantities x and y are liable to experimental error, or indeed that the linear relation between them is only approximately true. In such a case we can proceed as follows.

Assuming that the values of x_s are accurate we can derive the line of regression of y on x in the form

$$\frac{y - \bar{y}}{\sigma_Y} = r\frac{x - \bar{x}}{\sigma_X} \quad \text{or} \quad \frac{Y}{\sigma_Y} = r\frac{X}{\sigma_X}$$

Secondly, we can assume that the values of y_s are **accurate** and derive the line of regression of x on y in the form

$$\frac{x - \bar{x}}{\sigma_X} = r\frac{y - \bar{y}}{\sigma_Y} \quad \text{or} \quad \frac{X}{\sigma_X} = r\frac{Y}{\sigma_Y}$$

These equations are identical if $r = 1$. In general r is not equal to unity and the lines are not coincident; we choose the bisector of the acute angle between the lines as the line that best fits the data. It can be shown that $r^2 \leqslant 1$. If $r = 0$ the two lines of regression are parallel to the axes of x and y, that is, in general x and y are independent of one another. When $r^2 = 1$ all the points (x_s, y_s) lie on the coincident lines of regression and there is perfect correlation between x and y. The quantity r is known as the **coefficient of correlation** of x and y.

For the example discussed above the value of r may be found as follows, using $\bar{x} = 4 \cdot 5$ and $\bar{y} = 15 \cdot 1$.

x	X	XX	y	Y	YY	XY
0	$-4 \cdot 5$	$20 \cdot 25$	$4 \cdot 6$	$-10 \cdot 5$	$110 \cdot 25$	$47 \cdot 25$
1	$-3 \cdot 5$	$12 \cdot 25$	$7 \cdot 1$	$- 8 \cdot 0$	$64 \cdot 00$	$28 \cdot 00$
2	$-2 \cdot 5$	$6 \cdot 25$	$9 \cdot 5$	$- 5 \cdot 6$	$31 \cdot 36$	$14 \cdot 00$
3	$-1 \cdot 5$	$2 \cdot 25$	$11 \cdot 5$	$- 3 \cdot 6$	$12 \cdot 96$	$5 \cdot 40$
4	$-0 \cdot 5$	$0 \cdot 25$	$13 \cdot 7$	$- 1 \cdot 4$	$1 \cdot 96$	$0 \cdot 70$
5	$0 \cdot 5$	$0 \cdot 25$	$15 \cdot 9$	$0 \cdot 8$	$0 \cdot 64$	$0 \cdot 40$
6	$1 \cdot 5$	$2 \cdot 25$	$18 \cdot 6$	$3 \cdot 5$	$12 \cdot 25$	$5 \cdot 25$
7	$2 \cdot 5$	$6 \cdot 25$	$20 \cdot 9$	$5 \cdot 8$	$33 \cdot 64$	$14 \cdot 50$
8	$3 \cdot 5$	$12 \cdot 25$	$23 \cdot 5$	$8 \cdot 4$	$70 \cdot 56$	$29 \cdot 40$
9	$4 \cdot 5$	$20 \cdot 25$	$25 \cdot 4$	$10 \cdot 3$	$106 \cdot 09$	$46 \cdot 35$
sum 45	0	$82 \cdot 50$	$150 \cdot 7$	$- 0 \cdot 3$	$443 \cdot 71$	$191 \cdot 25$

Hence, $r = 191 \cdot 25 / \sqrt{(82 \cdot 50 \times 443 \cdot 71)} = 0 \cdot 999$. We note also that $[XY]/[XX] = 191 \cdot 25/82 \cdot 50 = 2 \cdot 32$ so that the relation between x and y is

$$y - 15 \cdot 1 = 2 \cdot 32(x - 4 \cdot 5)$$

or
$$y = 2 \cdot 32x + 4 \cdot 66$$

in keeping with the equation found earlier.

48. Accuracy of coefficients

It is clearly of some importance to be able to estimate the accuracy of the values of a and b derived by the method outlined above.

This can be done by applying the results discussed in Section 45. For using the values $y_1, y_2, \text{ - - -}, y_n$ and $x_1, x_2, \text{ - - -}, x_n$ and the most probable values of a and b, we can calculate the residuals d_s

given by $ax_s + b - y_s$. Then the mean square error α^2 in the expressions $ax_s + b - y_s$ is given by

$$\alpha^2 = [dd]/(n - 2)$$

Also, if α_a and α_b denote the standard errors in the values of a and b we have, using the normal equations (21) and (22),

$$\alpha_a^2/n = \alpha_b^2/[xx] = \alpha^2/\Delta$$

where Δ is the determinant

$$\begin{vmatrix} [xx] & [x] \\ [x] & n \end{vmatrix} = n[xx] - [x]^2$$

In the example considered above the normal equations are

$$285a + 45b = 869 \cdot 4$$
$$45b + 10b = 150 \cdot 7$$

leading to $a = 2 \cdot 32$ and $b = 4 \cdot 64$.

Hence we have $\alpha_a^2/10 = \alpha_b^2/285 = \alpha^2/825$

where $\alpha^2 = [dd]/8$ and $[dd] = 0 \cdot 3500$ as shown below.

x	y	d	dd
0	4·6	0·04	0·0016
1	7·1	−0·14	0·0196
2	9·5	−0·22	0·0484
3	11·5	0·10	0·0100
4	13·7	0·22	0·0484
5	15·9	0·34	0·1156
6	18·6	−0·04	0·0016
7	20·9	−0·02	0·0004
8	23·5	−0·30	0·0900
9	25·4	0·12	0·0144
sum 45	150·7		0·3500

Hence

$$\alpha_a = 0 \cdot 023 \qquad \text{and} \quad \alpha_b = 0 \cdot 123$$

We can therefore write

$$y = (2 \cdot 32 \pm 0 \cdot 02)x + 4 \cdot 64 \pm 0 \cdot 12$$

An alternative method has been given by Bond.[18]   If we write the relation $y = ax + b$ in the form $Y = aX$ where $Y = y - \bar{y}$ and $X = x - \bar{x}$ we have shown above that $a = [XY]/[XX]$.

Hence if the values of x_s are accurate and the standard error of the values of y_s (and therefore of the values of Y_s) is α we can write formally

$$a = [X(Y \pm \alpha)]/[XX]$$

which, using standard error (i) of Section 39, leads to

$$a = \frac{[XY] \pm \alpha\sqrt{[XX]}}{[XX]} = \frac{[XY]}{[XX]} \pm \frac{\alpha}{\sqrt{[XX]}}$$

Therefore the standard error of a is $\alpha_a = \alpha/\sqrt{[XX]}$.   This result is in keeping with that given above since

$$\frac{[XX]}{n} = \frac{[xx]}{n} - \bar{x}^2$$

that is,
$$n[XX] = n[xx] - [x]^2$$

and hence
$$\frac{\alpha_a^2}{n} = \frac{\alpha^2}{n[xx] - [x]^2}$$

Further, since $b = \bar{y} - a\bar{x}$ and the standard error of $\bar{y}$ is $\alpha/\sqrt{n}$ we can write

$$b = \bar{y} \pm \alpha/\sqrt{n} - (a \pm \alpha_a)\bar{x}$$

or
$$b = \bar{y} - a\bar{x} \pm \sqrt{\left(\frac{\alpha^2}{n} + \alpha_a^2\bar{x}^2\right)}$$

so that
$$\alpha_b^2 = \frac{\alpha^2}{n} + \alpha_a^2\bar{x}^2$$

$$= \frac{\alpha^2}{n} + \frac{\alpha_a^2[x]^2}{n^2}$$

$$= \alpha^2\frac{[xx]}{n[xx] - [x]^2}$$

as given above.

It is perhaps more convenient to write the equation in the form

$$Y \pm \alpha/\sqrt{n} = (a \pm \alpha_a)X$$

where

$Y = y - \bar{y}$, $X = x - \bar{x}$, $\alpha_a = \alpha/\sqrt{[XX]}$ and $\alpha^2 = [DD]/(n - 2)$, D_s being the value of $Y_s - aX_s$.

Thus in the example considered above we have found that $a = [XY]/[XX] = 191 \cdot 25/82 \cdot 50 = 2 \cdot 32$, and hence as shown below $[DD] = 0 \cdot 3580$.

X	Y	D	DD
$-4 \cdot 5$	$-10 \cdot 5$	$-0 \cdot 06$	$0 \cdot 0036$
$-3 \cdot 5$	$-8 \cdot 0$	$0 \cdot 12$	$0 \cdot 0144$
$-2 \cdot 5$	$-5 \cdot 6$	$0 \cdot 20$	$0 \cdot 0400$
$-1 \cdot 5$	$-3 \cdot 6$	$-0 \cdot 12$	$0 \cdot 0144$
$-0 \cdot 5$	$-1 \cdot 4$	$-0 \cdot 24$	$0 \cdot 0576$
$0 \cdot 5$	$0 \cdot 8$	$-0 \cdot 36$	$0 \cdot 1296$
$1 \cdot 5$	$3 \cdot 5$	$0 \cdot 02$	$0 \cdot 0004$
$2 \cdot 5$	$5 \cdot 8$	0	0
$3 \cdot 5$	$8 \cdot 4$	$0 \cdot 28$	$0 \cdot 0784$
$4 \cdot 5$	$10 \cdot 3$	$-0 \cdot 14$	$0 \cdot 0196$
sum			$0 \cdot 3580$

Hence

$$\alpha^2 = 0 \cdot 3580/8$$

therefore

$$\alpha_a^2 = 0 \cdot 3580/(8 \times 82 \cdot 50)$$
$$= 0 \cdot 000\,54$$

therefore

$$\alpha_a = 0 \cdot 023 \text{ as before.}$$

Also,

$$\frac{\alpha}{\sqrt{n}} = \sqrt{\frac{0 \cdot 3580}{80}} = 0 \cdot 067$$

Hence the relation is

$$Y \pm 0 \cdot 07 = (2 \cdot 32 \pm 0 \cdot 02)X$$

This can be written in terms of x and y as follows

$$(y - 15 \cdot 1) \pm 0 \cdot 07 = (2 \cdot 32 \pm 0 \cdot 02)(x - 4 \cdot 5)$$

therefore $y = (2 \cdot 32 \pm 0 \cdot 02)x + 4 \cdot 66 \pm \sqrt{[(0 \cdot 07)^2 + (0 \cdot 09)^2]}$

$$= (2 \cdot 32 \pm 0 \cdot 02)x + 4 \cdot 66 \pm 0 \cdot 12$$

in keeping with the result found earlier.

It might be added that if the observed values x_s, y_s are given the weight w_s the equations (21) and (22) above become

$$a[wxx] + b[wx] = [wxy]$$
$$a[wx] + b[w] = [wy]$$

so that

$$a = \frac{[w][wxy] - [wx][wy]}{[w][wxx] - [wx]^2}$$

and

$$b = \frac{[wy][wxx] - [wx][wxy]}{[w][wxx] - [wx]^2}$$

Also the standard errors of a and b are given by

$$\frac{\alpha_a^2}{[w]} = \frac{\alpha_b^2}{[wxx]} = \frac{\alpha^2}{[w][wxx] - [wx]^2}$$

where $\alpha^2 = [wdd]/(n - 2)$.

49. Other curves

It often happens that the relation between the two variables x and y is not linear. More generally, the relation may be of the form

$$y = a_0 + a_1 x + a_2 x^2 + \cdots + a_m x^m$$

involving $m + 1$ constants.

If n corresponding values of x and y are known, say, (x_s, y_s) with $s = 1, 2, 3, \cdots, n$ and $n > m + 1$, the values of the constants $a_0, a_1, a_2, \cdots, a_m$ may be chosen such that the sum of the squares given by

$$\sum_{s=1}^{n} (y_s - a_0 - a_1 x_s - a_2 x_s^2 \cdots - a_m x_s^m)^2$$

is least.

A particular example will illustrate the method.

If $y = a_0 + a_1 x + a_2 x^2$ we choose a_0, a_1, a_2 so that

$$\sum_{s=1}^{n} (y_s - a_0 - a_1 x_s - a_2 x_s^2)^2$$

is least.

Differentiating partially with respect to a_0, a_1, a_2 respectively we obtain the necessary conditions:

$$\Sigma(y_s - a_0 - a_1 x_s - a_2 x_s^2) = 0$$
$$\Sigma x_s(y_s - a_0 - a_1 x_s - a_2 x_s^2) = 0$$
$$\Sigma x_s^2(y_s - a_0 - a_1 x_s - a_2 x_s^2) = 0$$

The normal equations are therefore

$$[y] - na_0 - [x]a_1 - [xx]a_2 = 0$$
$$[xy] - [x]a_0 - [xx]a_1 - [xxx]a_2 = 0$$
$$[xxy] - [xx]a_0 - [xxx]a_1 - [xxxx]a_2 = 0$$

the solutions of which give the most probable values of a_0, a_1 and a_2.

Again, if we assume that the values of x_s are accurate and the values of y_s are subject to experimental error, the standard errors of the values of a_0, a_1, a_2 can be estimated by the method outlined in Section 45 above.

When the number of constants is large, the solution of the normal equations may be laborious. Special methods of solution have been devised.[19, 20]

The normal equations might more conveniently be written

$$s_0 a_0 + s_1 a_1 + s_2 a_2 = t_0$$
$$s_1 a_0 + s_2 a_1 + s_3 a_2 = t_1$$
$$s_2 a_0 + s_3 a_1 + s_4 a_2 = t_2$$

where
$$s_k = \sum_{r=1}^{n} x_r^k \quad \text{and} \quad t_k = \sum_{r=1}^{n} x_r^k y_r$$

The general form of these equations is obvious.

EXAMPLE

Fit a parabolic curve to the following data:

x	0	0·2	0·4	0·6	0·8	1·0	1·2
y	1·0	2·4	6·6	14·2	25·7	40·1	57·5

We assume that $y = a_0 + a_1X + a_2X^2$, where to simplify the arithmetic we take $X = 5x - 3$ and tabulate the working as follows.

X	y	X^2	X^3	X^4	Xy	X^2y	$y(calc)$	d	d^2
-3	$1 \cdot 0$	9	-27	81	$-3 \cdot 0$	$9 \cdot 0$	$1 \cdot 05$	$-0 \cdot 05$	$0 \cdot 0025$
-2	$2 \cdot 4$	4	-8	16	$-4 \cdot 8$	$9 \cdot 6$	$2 \cdot 22$	$0 \cdot 18$	$0 \cdot 0324$
-1	$6 \cdot 6$	1	-1	1	$-6 \cdot 6$	$6 \cdot 6$	$6 \cdot 69$	$-0 \cdot 09$	$0 \cdot 0081$
0	$14 \cdot 2$	0	0	0	0	0	$14 \cdot 46$	$-0 \cdot 26$	$0 \cdot 0676$
1	$25 \cdot 7$	1	1	1	$25 \cdot 7$	$25 \cdot 7$	$25 \cdot 54$	$0 \cdot 16$	$0 \cdot 0256$
2	$40 \cdot 1$	4	8	16	$80 \cdot 2$	$160 \cdot 4$	$39 \cdot 93$	$0 \cdot 17$	$0 \cdot 0289$
3	$57 \cdot 5$	9	27	81	$172 \cdot 5$	$517 \cdot 5$	$57 \cdot 62$	$-0 \cdot 12$	$0 \cdot 0144$
sum 0	$147 \cdot 5$	28	0	196	$264 \cdot 0$	$728 \cdot 8$			$0 \cdot 1795$

Hence the normal equations are

$$
\begin{aligned}
7a_0 \qquad\quad + 28a_2 &= 147 \cdot 5 \\
28a_1 \qquad\quad &= 264 \cdot 0 \\
28a_0 \qquad\quad + 196a_2 &= 728 \cdot 8
\end{aligned}
$$

leading to $a_0 = 14 \cdot 463$, $a_1 = 9 \cdot 428$ and $a_2 = 1 \cdot 652$.

Hence we have

$$
\begin{aligned}
y &= 14 \cdot 463 + 9 \cdot 428X + 1 \cdot 652X^2 \\
&= 14 \cdot 463 + 9 \cdot 428(5x - 3) + 1 \cdot 652(5x - 3)^2 \\
&= 1 \cdot 05 - 2 \cdot 42x + 41 \cdot 3x^2
\end{aligned}
$$

The uncertainties in the values of a_0, a_1, a_2 can be estimated as follows. We first find the residuals d given by $y - a_0 - a_1X - a_2X^2$ for the various values of X; these are tabulated above. We then calculate d^2 and find

$$
\alpha^2 = [dd]/(n - 3) = 0 \cdot 1795/4
$$

If the standard errors of a_0, a_1, a_2 are denoted by α_0, α_1, α_2 respectively, we have

$$
\frac{\alpha_0^2}{\begin{vmatrix} 28 & 0 \\ 0 & 196 \end{vmatrix}} = \frac{\alpha_1^2}{\begin{vmatrix} 7 & 28 \\ 28 & 196 \end{vmatrix}} = \frac{\alpha_2^2}{\begin{vmatrix} 7 & 0 \\ 0 & 28 \end{vmatrix}} = \frac{\alpha^2}{\begin{vmatrix} 7 & 0 & 28 \\ 0 & 28 & 0 \\ 28 & 0 & 196 \end{vmatrix}}
$$

therefore
$$\frac{\alpha_0^2}{112} = \frac{\alpha_1^2}{12} = \frac{\alpha_2^2}{4} = \frac{0 \cdot 1795/4}{336}$$

therefore $\alpha_0 = \pm 0 \cdot 122, \quad \alpha_1 = \pm 0 \cdot 040, \quad \alpha_2 = \pm 0 \cdot 023$

Hence

$$y = 14 \cdot 463 \pm 0 \cdot 122 + (9 \cdot 428 \pm 0 \cdot 040)X + (1 \cdot 652 \pm 0 \cdot 023)X^2$$

The simplification of this expression is complex, since α_0, α_1, α_2 are not independent. If, however, we treat them as independent we get

$$y = 1 \cdot 05 \pm 0 \cdot 27 - (2 \cdot 42 \pm 0 \cdot 72)x + (41 \cdot 3 \pm 0 \cdot 6)x^2$$

The standard error $0 \cdot 27$ is overestimated, but the others are satisfactory.

EXERCISES 6

1. From the equations
   $$3x + y = 2 \cdot 9, \quad x - 2y = 0 \cdot 9 \quad \text{and} \quad 2x - 3y = 1 \cdot 9$$
   find the most probable values of x and y.

2. The equations
   $$x - 3y = -5 \cdot 6$$
   $$4x + y = 8 \cdot 1$$
   and $$2x - y = 0 \cdot 5$$

   have weights 1, 2, 3 respectively. Find the most probable values of x and y, and their standard errors.

3. Independent sets of observations led to the results
   $$u = 1 \cdot 23 \pm 0 \cdot 06, \quad v = 2 \cdot 17 \pm 0 \cdot 08$$
   $$\text{and} \quad u + v = 3 \cdot 50 \pm 0 \cdot 12.$$
   Find the most probable values of u and v and their standard errors.

4. Find the most probable values of x, y and z that satisfy the equations
   $$x + y + z = 4 \cdot 01, \quad 2x - y + z = 1 \cdot 04,$$
   $$x + 3y - 2z = 5 \cdot 02 \quad \text{and} \quad 3x + y = 4 \cdot 97$$
   assuming the equations have equal weight. Find also the standard errors of x, y and z.

5. Find the most probable position of the point of which the measured distances from the points $(1, 0)$, $(3, 1)$ and $(-1, 2)$ are respectively $3 \cdot 1$, $2 \cdot 2$ and $3 \cdot 2$ units. Estimate the uncertainties in the co-ordinates of the point.

6. The three angles of a plane triangle are measured and found to be

$$A = 48° \, 5' \, 10'', \quad B = 60° \, 25' \, 24'' \quad \text{and} \quad C = 70° \, 42' \, 7''.$$

Find the most probable values of A, B and C assuming that the measurements have (i) equal weights, and (ii) weights 1, 2, 3 respectively.

7. Plot the values of x and y given in the example discussed in Section 46 and draw the best straight line through them. Find the equation of the line drawn.

Find the values of a and b using only the values (i) $x = 0$, 1, 2, 3, 4, 5 and the corresponding values of y, and (ii) $x = 5$, 6, 7, 8, 9 and the corresponding values of y.

8. Two quantities D and d are measured as follows:

d (in.)	$\frac{1}{2}$	$\frac{3}{4}$	1	$1\frac{1}{4}$	$1\frac{1}{2}$	$1\frac{3}{4}$	2
D (in.)	$1 \cdot 19$	$1 \cdot 31$	$1 \cdot 42$	$1 \cdot 52$	$1 \cdot 64$	$1 \cdot 76$	$1 \cdot 87$

Show that they satisfy approximately a relation of the form $D = ad + b$, find the most probable values of a and b, and estimate the errors in those values.

9. Fit a linear relation to the following data and estimate the errors in the values of the constants obtained.

x	10	12	13	17	19	20
y	$11 \cdot 0$	$7 \cdot 6$	$6 \cdot 2$	$-0 \cdot 1$	$-3 \cdot 2$	$-5 \cdot 0$

10. Values of the surface tension of water, $\gamma \, \text{N m}^{-1}$, at different temperatures, $t°\,\text{C}$, are given below. If $\gamma = a - b\theta$, where θ is the temperature on the Kelvin scale, find the most probable values of a and b.

t	10	20	30	40	50	60
$\gamma \times 10^3$	$74 \cdot 22$	$72 \cdot 75$	$71 \cdot 18$	$69 \cdot 56$	$67 \cdot 91$	$66 \cdot 18$

11. Values of the surface tension of bromobenzene, γ N m^{-1}, at different temperatures, $t°$ C, are given below. Fit a law of the form $\gamma = \gamma_0[1 - (\theta/670)]^n$ where θ is the temperature in degrees Kelvin.

t	15	42	49	78	90	105	125
$\gamma \times 10^3$	37·92	34·92	33·78	30·73	29·30	27·62	25·30

12. Using the values of the velocity of light c given in question 10 of Exercises 5, use the method of least squares to show that c is related to the epoch D by the relation

$$c = 299\,777 \cdot 27 \pm 2 \cdot 03 - (0 \cdot 381 \pm 0 \cdot 234)(D - 1930)$$

May it be concluded that there is experimental evidence of a linear variation of c with time?

13. Fit a parabolic curve to the data given in the example discussed in Section 49, but excluding the value $x = 1 \cdot 2$. Use the calculated expression for y to find y when $x = 1 \cdot 2$.

14. Values of the viscosity of water, η Ns m^{-2}, at different temperatures, $t°$ C, are given below. Fit a law of the form $\eta^{-1} = a + bt + ct^2$.

t	10	20	30	40	50	60	70
$\eta \times 10^3$	1·308	1·005	0·801	0·656	0·549	0·469	0·406

15. Assuming that $\eta = Ae^{k/T}$ where T is the temperature on the Kelvin scale, use the data given in question 14 above to find the most probable values of A and k.

REFERENCES

(1) BULLARD, E. C. *Phil. Trans A*, **235**, pp. 445–531 (1936).

(2) HEYL, P. R. *Bur. Stand. J. Res.* (Washington), **5**, p. 1243 (1930).

(3) SCRASE, F. J. *Quart. J. Roy. Meteorol. Soc.*, **61**, pp. 368–378 (1935).

(4) AITKEN, A. C. *Statistical Mathematics*, p. 72 (Edinburgh: Oliver and Boyd Ltd., 1952).

(5) RUTHERFORD, E., and GEIGER, H. *Phil. Mag.*, **20**, pp. 698–707 (1910).

(6) JEFFREYS, H. *Theory of Probability* (Oxford: Clarendon Press, 1948).

(7) WHITTAKER, E. T., and ROBINSON, G. *Calculus of Observations*, p. 179 (London: Blackie and Son Ltd., 1929).

(8) See ref. (7), p. 177.

(9) JEFFREYS, H. *Phil. Trans A*, **237**, pp. 231–271 (1938).

(10) BESSEL, F. W. *Astron. Nachr.*, **15**, Nr. 358–359.

(11) HANSMANN, G. H. *Biometrika*, **26**, pp. 128–195 (1934).

(12) BIRGE, R. T. *Rep. Progr. Phys.*, **8**, p. 95 (1941).

(13) BIRGE, R. T. *Phys. Rev.*, **40**, pp. 207–227 (1932).

(14) See ref. (7), p. 175.

(15) WEATHERBURN, C. E. *Mathematical Statistics*, p. 188 (London: Cambridge University Press, 1952).

(16) See ref. (7), p. 174.

(17) See ref. (7), p. 243 and later.

(18) BOND, W. N. *Probability and Random Errors*, p. 96 (London: Edward Arnold and Co. Ltd., 1935).

(19) HARTREE, D. R. *Numerical Analysis* (Oxford: Clarendon Press, 1952).

(20) MILNE, W. E *Numerical Calculus* (Princeton University Press, 1950).

BIBLIOGRAPHY

The following is a list of works on statistics and theory of errors which, it is hoped, might serve as some guide to students through a very extensive literature. The works range from the most elementary to the very advanced and are quoted in their approximate order of difficulty.

Statistics and statistical mathematics

MORONEY. *Facts from Figures* (London: Penguin Books Ltd., 1951).

AITKEN. *Statistical Mathematics* (Edinburgh: Oliver and Boyd Ltd., 1952).

WEATHERBURN. *Mathematical Statistics* (London: Cambridge University Press, 1952).

LEVY and ROTH. *Elements of Probability* (London: Oxford University Press, 1951).

JEFFREYS. *Theory of Probability* (Oxford: Clarendon Press, 1948).

Errors of observation and related topics

BOND. *Probability and Random Errors* (London: Edward Arnold and Co. Ltd., 1935).

BRADDICK. *The Physics of Experimental Method* (London: Chapman and Hall Ltd.).

WHITTAKER and ROBINSON. *Calculus of Observations* (London: Blackie and Son Ltd., 1929).

DEMING and BIRGE. *Rev. Mod. Phys.*, **6**, p. 119 (1934).

LYON. Dealing with data (Oxford: Pergamon Press, 1970).

SMART. *Combination of Observations* (London: Cambridge University Press, 1958).

INDEX